Weight Loss Script
Pre-talk & Hypnosis
Psychotherapy & Hypnotherapy
Neuro-Linguistic Programming (NLP)
Cognitive Behavioural Therapy (CBT)
Clinical Psychology

By
David Glenn

I am dedicating this book to my clients, in appreciation.
Thank you, because without you I would never have had the experience,
and therefore the knowledge, to write this book.
David Glenn.

<u>Disclaimer, Legal Warning and Notice</u>

The CD Rom that is mentioned in this book is given to those studying as a Diploma with me personally. It is not given out for free with this book.

☐

Contents

Introduction

THOSE STUDENTS THAT HAVE READ MY BOOK: "Beginner to Advanced Practitioner Training Course & Self Development in Psychotherapy Hypnotherapy Neuro-Linguistic Programming (NLP) Cognitive Behavioural Therapy (CBT) Clinical Psychology Vol: 1" will not need to read this book. The information within this book has already been covered in the book just mentioned. Even so, I have also published this script as a separate digital book for those people that requested me to do so.

This book is more than just a weight loss script I will also give many examples of real clients that I treated in therapy. I will show you how I structure a set plan for a therapy session, and of what needs to be done to help the client overcome their problem. Also I will explain to you the knowledge that the client needs to be educated on, in order to help them further. Even though I have a set plan, please remember to always personalise a session to the client within the plan.

The script in this book has been written in a way, not intended to be read out to the clients, word for word. I simply want to show you different beginners and advanced ways of conducting therapy, in a structured session that you can personalise to each client. I have written both the pre-talk and what is said under hypnosis to the client far longer than it need be. I have done this purposely, to give you more examples of what can be said, so that you can pick and choose what you feel fits that particular client best. So, once again, please note that this script is not intended to be read word for word to the client. It can even be used in a number of sessions, if needed, to make each session different from the previous.

I am David Glenn, a Professional Psychotherapist, Hypnotherapist, NLP Practitioner and Trainer with over twenty year's experience in this profession. I have written this book to pass on my knowledge for those:

1) Interested in the cognitive psychology of oneself as a self-development help guide in understanding and utilising the power of your own mind to overcome: Weight Gain, in order to get the best out of your life by being slimmer and fitter.

2) Wanting to have a successful career in Hypnotherapy, Neuro-Linguistic Programming (NLP), Cognitive Behavioural Therapy (CBT), Life Coaching and Psychotherapy as a whole. Developing or enhancing your therapy skills in dealing with low self-esteem clients with a weight gain problem, to help them recover their cognitive, and physical health, as well as their wellbeing.

Everybody can study this script course book as home study training. It is laid out in layman's terms, so those with no previous knowledge of the subject, can still learn how to use the power of your own mind to enrich your life. Even if you do not want to be a Professional Therapist, you can still study this course to understand yourself more, for self-help and personal development. This will enable you to break negative habits, and have unlimited confidence with the techniques that you can learn and use in your life, or therapy practice to improve your psyche, or that of a client's cognitive health (psychological health) and wellbeing. You will also learn how to hypnotise your clients, friends and family, and find the beneficial power of self-hypnosis.

Enrich your knowledge and skills with what I am going to teach you, which can be used in general life, for yourself and others, or by those wishing a new profession in Hypnotherapy, CBT, NLP Practitioner or Psychotherapist. Keep an open mind to new possibilities. How you have thought, communicated, and acted throughout life, may need to change, or be adapted for positive effect. I will teach you the tools of how this can be done to enable you or others to move on positively in life.

Once you have read and fully understood this book, for many people it is a life changing experience. My philosophy on therapy and psychology in general is - it is the art of understanding the psychology of people, our behaviour, the mind model, body language, communication and speech. You will be able to understand how your mind works, and how to utilise its power for positive change.

Anyone on earth, if able bodied, can drive, or learn to drive a car. Be that as it may, that does not mean you will ever be a professional rally, or formula one racing car driver. In order to be the formula one expert in the psychotherapy world, you have to have that special something: innate quality. You cannot think, act, or communicate as the general public do. In general life, what you think is rude, morally wrong, or what you would not dream of saying to a fellow human being in public, those same rules do not apply in the therapy room, because the client is paying you for a highly skilled service. You must never allow your own personality to effect what needs to be done, in order to help the client progress forwards positively in their lives. Conducting therapy is not about you or your beliefs; it is about what is best for the client, even if you have to be cruel to be kind, and go outside of your comfort zone. You may have thought that therapy is just about counselling, empathy, listening, understanding, relating to, comforting and simply relaxing a person. It is far more complex than that. You are not there to comfort a client; you are there to enable them to become unstuck, get out from their negative mindset, and move forward for positive effect and self-fulfilment. You are there to enable them to see the wood from the trees, so they can find the truth about themselves. Thereby you can support them with education, by imparting psychotherapy knowledge that can be adapted, to enable growth and movement. You will understand this more as you learn, by reading through this book in full.

I have met many students that have all the knowledge they require to be great Hypnotherapist, CBT, NLP Therapists, but yet many lack intuition. This is a skill that you either already have, or you have not. Without it, success as a psychotherapist will be limited. Of course I have also met many students that have no confidence whatsoever, and I watch them grow and develop into great therapists through the knowledge from my training.

I have a very modern approach to therapy for today's generation, as I am sure you will come to realise as we continue. Once you have absorbed all the knowledge I am about to teach you, you will know more than most therapists that have been in the profession for many years. This book contains valuable information on conducting a therapy session as a Professional Hypnotherapist, and Psychotherapist, despite that I still advise all my students to practise on volunteers, for charities, family and friends, before their first paying client. Conducting psychotherapy is an extremely complex and skilful job. Therefore after reading this book, and gaining some practical skills, if you do not feel you have the ability to put in place the knowledge I have imparted in this book, then I will teach you the skills in a group or one on one setting. Through tailor-made training this will enable you to set up in business, with the greatest confidence in knowledge and skills to succeed in a successful psychotherapy career.

Prepare yourself for a truly amazing, life-changing experience. Enjoy as you learn, and I guarantee, at times you will be thinking: WOW! MIND BLOWING, INSPIRATIONAL KNOWLEDGE AND WISDOM, ALL IN THIS BOOK!

My recommendation is to read this book, in its entirety, more than once, to fully understand the connection between each skill being taught. Please do not speed read this book, or skip chapters. Take your time to absorb all the information being taught.

It will also be most beneficial to put the knowledge and skills into practise, by attending my group training workshop sessions or one to one training.

☐

The Workings of the Mind Model Bulletin Points

AS A STUDENT, before you conduct a therapy session with any type of client, you first must learn the mind model and memorise it. I have added the bulletin points of the Mind Model in this chapter to help you.

Three parts of the whole mind:

1) Conscious Mind Functions: Rational logical thought - Makes decisions, but the subconscious determines on whether those decisions are carried out or not - One task at once - Willpower - General speech.

2) Subconscious Mind Functions: Many tasks at once - Memories - Imagination - Emotions - Habits - Protects us - In control - Intelligence - Perception of reality - Habitual speech.

3) Analytical or Critical Area: This part of the mind is the conduit connection between the conscious and subconscious, passing information between the two main parts of the whole mind. It is the part of the mind that reasons to determine new information as being fact or fiction (real or fake), based on information from the subconscious memories.

The subconscious four reference points:

(A) The subconscious mind does not know the difference between what is real or imagined.
(B) The subconscious also does not know the difference between good habits, or bad habits. A habit is a habit through repetition regardless.
(C) The subconscious has no concept of time, past, present or future with regards to associated links.
(D) The subconscious also works via associated links, which are memories, cognitive thought (a persons perception of fact or fiction, real or fake, true or false-truth), and emotions (pain or pleasure), that are associated (connected), within the mind to an anchor. This can be any sound, touch, taste, smell, or seeing a certain person (or behaviour), colour, object or place.

The seven mind rules:

1) Ideas or thoughts result in physical immediate emotional reactions.
2) The subconscious mind delivers what we focus on.
3) Repeated negative or positive focused thoughts result in long-term organic change over time.
4) Imagination overpowers knowledge within in the mind.
5) Fixed thoughts can only be replaced by another via the subconscious.
6) Opposing ideas cannot be held at the same time.
7) Conscious effort alone, results in opposite subconscious success.

Seven Important Mind Rules

MOST PEOPLE WRONGLY BELIEVE that the mind and body are two separate things, but the brain is part of the body as a whole, and the mind is part of the brain. You are one being, so the mind and body are the same whole, because they are connected.

☐

One: Ideas or thoughts result in physical immediate emotional reactions - Thought processes affect the reactions of your immediate behaviour, even if you are not consciously aware of your reaction. For example, a micro-signal in the facial area of looking upset. Negative thoughts of any kind develop instantly into negative, physical, emotional changes within the body. Example: blushing, or imagining being upset, or crying in a certain situation, will result in you doing so, by just the thought of being confronted by that situation. If you imagine a spider is going to hurt you, then the imagined idea causes a physical, emotional, negative reaction to fear, even though the spider is of no danger to you and may not even be there. Thoughts that release powerful emotions, whether real or imagined will, without fail, seep into subconscious mind. Physical, emotional reactions then occur, due to the subconscious accepting the negative thoughts as fact. This is due to the subconscious mind not knowing the difference between what is real or imagined. Of course happy thoughts also have an instant effect on your emotions, and therefore your body as well, by having a positive effect on the body unlike negative thoughts. Consider the mind and body as being the same thing, because the mind is part of the body, therefore whatever thought you have, affects every living cell within your body, either negatively or positively, depending on your thought, so it's best to think positively.

Two: The subconscious mind delivers what we focus on - When wanting to achieve a realistic goal that you are not already doing, if you focus your subconscious mind on a negative, then a negative result is what will be achieved and the goal is failed. Alternatively, by playing a positive movie of achieving that same goal within your imagination, then you will achieve that goal on a conscious level, because your subconscious mind believes you have already achieved it, and that makes it easier to do so via the subconscious auto pilot. The reason the subconscious believes you have already achieved the goal, is because you played the positive movie of doing so, and the subconscious mind does not know the difference between what is real or imagined, because both are your reality. You made a conscious decision to do something, your subconscious then plays a positive movie of what you consciously want to achieve, and by doing so, it makes a task easier to achieve, due to the two parts of the mind working in agreement, instead of being in conflict.

What I have just written above, is in relation to a person that wants to achieve a goal that they should be doing, but are not doing it. However, a person with a bad habit is the opposite, because they are already doing something that they should not be doing, so the focus of the subconscious mind has to be different. A person with a bad habit wrongly focuses the subconscious mind with the association of pleasure to the habit, this positive association must be changed to a negative focused association, in order to stop the bad habit. We are often asked, "Who are you?" The simple answer is to tell the questioner your name. However, that does not really tell them who you are. The real answer is, "I am what I focus my subconscious mind on."

Three: Repeated negative or positive focused thoughts result in long-term organic change over time - When ill, negative, repeated, focused thoughts you have about yourself delay the healing process, and can even kill you with stress due to causing heart failure. When positive with uplifting thoughts, we tend to recover faster from illness. This is the mind and body connection being the same thing. A large percentage of human illnesses are functional as opposed to organic, so continued, negative, focused thoughts that you have about yourself, result in long-term, organic, negative change and therefore illness. The term used is

"Psychosomatic" (illness caused by the mind).So, mind rule one and two develops into mind rule three, if the person continues the negative thoughts about them self. People that cause illness through the mind can be classed as neurotic, and the term used for a person that continuously has psychosomatic illness is a hypochondriac. Even though some people have genuine diseases, negative, repeated, focused thoughts will still result in further negative long-term organic change over time. With the use of hypnosis, the effect from the negative, focused thought can be changed, by changing the thought to positive. Be that as it may, a negative thought can also result in positive, organic change. For example: a negative thought towards the bad habit of over eating, means the organic change is better for long-term health due to the client avoiding excessive amounts of food. Of course positive focused thoughts result in long-term positive health benefits for the mind and body.

Four: Imagination overpowers knowledge within in the mind - A person that is overweight has the conscious knowledge that eating junk is killing them, but yet they have not imagined the negative effects within the subconscious mind. The subconscious mind is therefore still playing a positive, imagined, associated movie toward the bad habit, and therefore the person does not change, because imagination has overpowered their knowledge, even though the positive association to the habit is wrong and is killing them. Once again remember that imagination (subconscious mind), is more powerful than knowledge (conscious mind), and the subconscious always wins, even when wrong. In order to do anything in life, you have to first imagine doing it, hence why imagination (subconscious mind), is more powerful than knowledge (conscious mind), within the whole mind. This is why people fail, they have made a conscious decision for change, and then tried to consciously succeed, but it is impossible to consciously lose weight, or any bad habit, when the subconscious is still playing a positive movie towards the bad habit. Change the positive to a negative within the subconscious and the bad habit is avoided. With regards to people with depression, anxiety, stress, low confidence etc, the movie within their subconscious is of wrongly believing an imagined, negative thought as fact. Example: a person may imagine that it is fact that they are useless, ugly etc, so they feel depressed and fear, even though they are wrong, but the negative, imagined thought is fact in their warped perception of reality. Change the imagined thought to agree with logic knowledge, and the person's reality changes for the positive and the problem is solved.

Five: Fixed thoughts can only be replaced by another via the subconscious - If every morning at 7am I got up and consciously made the decision to tap my head three times with my hand, the subconscious, eventually through repetition, takes the task on as a habit, it has become a fixed thought and it is incorporated into my morning ritual. This habit would then be protected by the subconscious. So to get up one morning and consciously force myself not to tap my head, would result in an overwhelming urge of anxiety, as if something is wrong, as if there is a potential danger. This anxiety of feeling there is a danger, is simply the subconscious mind reminding me to do the habit, because it wrongly feels it is doing me a favour protecting that habit, by keeping me from harm.

In order to overcome this anxiety, and to stop a potential danger, be it real or not, the subconscious reminds me of the habit, so I tap my head for instant relief from anxiety. In other words there is a subconscious resistance to change because the subconscious mind believes it is doing me a favour, so continues to protect the habit even though it is not healthy to do so. Remember the subconscious does not know the difference between a good or bad habit, it protects it regardless, as if there is a danger not to do so. It is simply an associated link between getting up in the morning and tapping my head that became a habit. In other words, repetition that has become a habit through an associated link. Changing the associated link subconsciously, will bring about permanent results.

For example, imagining myself getting up in the morning and doing press-ups, this would occupy my hands so as not to tap my head, and over time the press-ups become a new more positive habit. This is why a person that over eats always wants snacks at certain times of the day or night, due to the association of a certain time or place, to eating. They have never imagined doing something else and not eating.

Dear student, as far as the subconscious mind is concerned, what is the difference between the habit of over eating and the habit of me tapping my head? Think about that for a moment.

The answer is no difference, because both habits are protected within the subconscious, both create anxiety if not carried out, they are in fact the same. A habit. So now let me ask, what is the difference between over eating and swimming within the subconscious? The answer is they are the same, because both habits are protected, because the subconscious mind does not know the difference between swimming and the habit of over eating, both are a habit regardless of them being good or bad. The habit of swimming is protected to stop you from the danger of drowning if you fall in to a river, and the habit of eating junk is protected to save you from potential danger that's not real. Your subconscious doesn't know there is no danger by not binge eating, because the overweight person has never told the subconscious mind of the danger of doing the habit in the first place. They have associated pleasure to it, so of course they keep eating junk. The fixed thought that needs to be changed, needs to be replaced via the subconscious, because that is where the habit is stored, and not in the conscious mind, so of course consciously wanting to change will always result in failure, due to mind rule four: "Imagination overpowers knowledge within in the mind", and a combination of the other mind rules. You are starting to see how these seven mind rules are all connected, and of course they are, because we only have one mind each.

Six: Opposing ideas cannot be held at the same time - This means that once the subconscious has accepted an idea as fact, then any opposing conscious ideas will always be rejected. The subconscious, always conflicts against an opposing idea from the conscious mind, and as you know the subconscious is the stronger part of the mind and therefore, overpowers the opposing conscious idea or thought. That is true unless you change an idea on a subconscious level so that both parts of the mind are in agreement. For example: a person consciously thinks "I want to eating junk", but they continue to because their subconscious is protecting the habit and positive associated links of eating junk, due to them not showing their subconscious any differently. Remember mind rule four: "Imagination overpowers knowledge within in the mind", which means the subconscious overpowers the conscious, and that of course has a detrimental effect on a person's life, and that is why, in order to change, it has to be done subconsciously first, to then be a conscious act. Also the subconscious cannot have two opposing ideas at the same time, for example: it cannot think fact (real) and fiction (not real), towards an idea at the same time, it is one or the other idea. The same with the conscious mind, you cannot logically think something is true and false at the same time. Nonetheless as you now know, the conscious can try to oppose an idea from the subconscious, but again, two opposing ideas cannot be held at the same time, so the stronger more powerful subconscious wins.

Seven: Conscious effort alone, results in opposite subconscious success - Conscious effort alone, results in opposite, subconscious success, means that; if you only consciously attempt to try and achieve your goal, you will fail every time. For example: a weight loss client consciously thinks, "I don't want that chocolate bar because I don't need it." They have, by doing so, implanted within the subconscious mind, an image of them wanting it and eating it, the exact opposite of the conscious thought. So the client then eats the chocolate due to the powerful suggestion of the image in their subconscious mind of doing so. If you say to yourself consciously "Don't think of a black cat", then subconsciously you have thought of one, the opposite of what you wanted to achieve. This is why conscious effort alone will never work to overcome a problem, and as you now know, the subconscious is more powerful than the conscious, and it overpowers the conscious will every time. This is why hypnosis is so successful in helping people overcome any problem.

Successful Weight Loss Session Explained

A SUCCESSFUL WEIGHT LOSS SESSION is broken down into three parts:

a) Pre-talk
b) Suggestibility test
c) Hypnosis session

Examples of Real Weight Loss Clients

Before I explain the pre-talk, I will give you real examples of what weight loss clients have said to me in the therapy room. They make up excuses within their own mind in order to justify overeating, as the excuses and lies temporarily takes away their guilt of abusing their own body, which also gives them a deluded sense of control over the problem. In other words their actions of gross overeating, or eating foods that they know are harmful for them, are wrongly justified by their excuses and lies to themselves. This of course is delusional and most of the time they are not aware of the lies they tell themselves, until I point them out to the client. Please note that these are all true examples and they are not made up. A client said to me: "I buy chocolate and biscuits for my partner, because it wouldn't be fair if I didn't, because he isn't on a diet." That was habitual speech from a false-truth thought.

I then asked: "Does your partner eat chocolate?" "Not that often," she replied, but yet the client buys chocolate every day or week as if buying the junk for her partner, when in fact she eats it and not him. She was using her partner as an excuse to abuse her own body, instead of taking responsibility for her own actions. Therefore what she had told me was said via habitual speech, and not general speech. It took away her guilt and gave her a deluded sense of control over her weight problem, but she was not aware of this until I told her.

Clients use kidology on themselves to justify buying the chocolate in the first place, because it took away their guilt of buying it and then eating it. I have had many clients say to me similar things as this client had said, and many others have said: "I lost four pounds two weeks ago, so I can now treat myself to chocolate." Weight loss clients will go and join a gym, or buy a bike or some other form of exercise equipment for the home, and then only use it twice. Again they have done this to kid themselves into thinking they are doing themselves a favour, it takes away their guilt when they binge eat, or snack, because they lie to themselves that the junk is justified because tomorrow they will be on the exercise equipment, when in fact they won't be. They will tell you: "I go to the gym" when in fact they have only been twice. "I've got a bike" some say, but they never use it etc. I have even had clients tell me that they take their gym clothes to work with them every day, but after work they just go home. The thought of going to the gym gave them a moment of pleasure, again, using kidology on themselves, when in fact they had no intensions of going to exercise.

Every January, weight loss clients say: "Right, new year's resolution for me, I'm going to get fit and slim." They start off with good intentions and then the excuses start. They say to themselves: "Well that wedding I'm going to a month from now, a big buffet will be on, so I'll go on a diet after that." One excuse after another, throughout the year, and before they know it the year has passed and nothing has been done, so their health worsens. I have even had a client say to me: "I can't start a diet today because it's too cold outside." Another said: "I was going to start a diet last week, but I couldn't because it was Monday." At the time of making the excuse, which is habitual speech, the client wrongly believes it is a totally normal, expectable thing to say, but as you know that is their warped sense of their own reality, which must be changed. The client needs to be told how ridiculous these excuses are by ridiculing the thought, which then prevents them from making excuses later. Show them within their subconscious the negative outcome to the excuses. Please note that you are ridiculing the excuse and not the client.

"I like the taste of food" they say, but yet they do not even chew it, they wolf it down and it has not even touched the sides of their mouth. The next bite is ready to shovel in even before they have finished the first bite, one load after another, into the mouth, so they don't even have the food on their taste buds long enough to fully enjoy the flavour, so again, another excuse. I always remind the client that taste buds are in their mouth, and not in their gut. Added to this, if the client genuinely only over ate the foods they liked, then why are they only over eating junk that piles the weight on and not healthy foods that they also enjoy the taste of? They like the taste of bananas etc but yet they do not over eat those foods that are good for them, so for a client to use the excuse: "I like the taste of food" then only ever eat junk, is obviously a delusional excuse to take away their guilt of self-abuse. Once I make the clients aware of their excuses, then the excuses can no longer be used without a sense of guilt by thinking of the excuse. Most weight loss clients have never even processed the thought that what they are doing is self-abuse. Once told, an abreaction can occur for positive change.

On a Friday they say: "I'll start the diet on Monday," Habitual speech from a false-truth that again takes away their guilt of binge eating over the weekend. Monday comes, and no diet is started, but on the previous Friday, the lie they told themselves made them feel good as a deluded, short lived fix, that later creates more guilt by them having not carrying out what they promised them self. So then that guilt of failure depresses them, so then they use the depressed state as an excuse for a treat and so the cycle continues of eating junk as a deluded comfort.

Clients previous to a session cook too much food for one sitting and then tell themselves: "I'll eat the rest another day," even though they eat it all at once and are bursting because they are so full. They say (habitual speech): "I'm eating these crisps and chocolate as a treat, because I've had a stressful day at work." The fact is, they eat that junk every day, so again they need a new excuse. A treat is something we do every blue moon, not every day and justify it with a lie. We all get stressed, but that does not mean we go and abuse ourselves and the clients must be told that. If work is not used as an excuse, then it is the kid's fault, or the partner's etc, always an external source and never their fault in their deluded warped minds. It is regular for clients to blame others for their weight gain, and as another true example: a male client used his wife as an excuse, by putting the blame on her of his own self-abuse, just like a child would when blaming others when they have been naughty, when in fact he was the one in the wrong. He said (habitual speech): "My problem is she cooks and piles it on the plate."

Another client told me: "My boyfriend is bigger than me and we eat at the same time, so I have to have the same amount of food as him." Of course that is not a logical thing to say, which is a false-truth said via habitual speech, and the same can be said for all weight loss client's excuses, but yet to them it is a totally normal way of thinking, until I change their way of thinking and their behaviour. Others say: "I'm not going to have time to eat later" that gives the client an excuse to binge eat, but yet when later comes, they still make time for more food. This client was blaming: "Time" and "Work" for their self-abuse, again instead of taking responsibility for their own destructive behaviour. One client said: "Unfortunately my mother eats chocolate, so I tend to as well," of course this client was taking away their guilt by blaming their own mother, even though she was not being force fed by her mother.

This example is a male client that gained weight by drinking too much alcohol. He told me: "I have to go to the pub every day because that is where I do my crossword puzzles." He was blaming over drinking on a puzzle, when he could have done the puzzle in his own home, or still at the pub, but without an alcoholic drink, however in his warped reality he had never considered that. He then said: "Being ex-forces, drinking is in our culture." The fact is, it had been over twenty years since he had left the forces, but yet he was still using it has an excuse. Remember the subconscious has no concept of time, so his subconscious mind was talking to me; therefore he had no real conscious perception of how ridiculous his excuses were. So this client had two main excuses for his weight gain, those of blaming a puzzle as if it was law that he had to also drink whilst doing a puzzle, which is an associated link between puzzle and drink, and the other excuse was of blaming his past of having been in the forces. Ridiculous excuses for him to think that way, but obvious to us once I bring it to your attention, but again to the client, it is wrongly seen as a normal, rational way of thinking. Once I made the client aware of his childlike excuses he stopped going to the pub drinking and he lost weight.

A male client told me: "My problem is at work, if someone brings a packet of biscuits in I just can't leave them alone, I just can't." This client was blaming work colleagues for his weight gain, the same as a child blames others when being naughty, even though he is an adult this is therefore a childlike mentality. Another client said: "The kids keep throwing things into the trolley." This client was blaming the kids, even though it was her that paid for all the junk food. Notice the client used the word: "Things" and not specifically: "Chocolate" or "Crisps" and that is because she didn't want to see the true situation in her mind, because she would have been ashamed. Of course I lead her towards an abreaction of being ashamed within the session to then associate the emotional shame to buying and eating junk (anchor). One client said: "I have nothing to do with my hands anymore because I have recently stopped smoking, so I pick at food all day." I asked the client when had she stopped smoking and it was two and a half years ago, so not recent at all, so once again, a client blaming an external source for their self-abuse, and in this case stopping smoking. "I had a bad knee so couldn't get about much," this client used the words: "Had" and "Couldn't", as in past tense, so this told me that the original knee problem had healed but yet she was still using it as an excuse to over eat. I made the client aware of this and she agreed that it had healed. In her mind she then had to find another delusional excuse to justify herself-abuse so she said: "My knee has got worse since I put weight on, so I still can't get about much." So even though the original knee problem had healed which she admitted to, she had created another problem due to the extra weight pressure on her knee, she thought she could use this as an excuse, but I quickly turned it around by making her aware that by losing the weight the knee will be fine.

"I have an underactive thyroid gland so that puts weight on me," a client said, so I delved deeper and asked her had her medical condition been diagnosed by a doctor and she said: "Yes it's just on the border line." I said: "So in this case it is not underactive at all, because it is only border line underactive," she agreed but then said: "Well yes but it is boarder line so it could be." This client was using a medical condition that she did not have, as an excuse of gaining weight, even though over eating, drinking and lack of movement (exercise) are the only things that gain us weight. Some excuses that clients give can be comical, for example, a client's excuse for not exercising was: "I bought a cross trainer but it's now a clothes peg, so I can't train on it," when the client said that, she was not joking because to her, that was a serious, rational statement. Some clients will randomly say things as if it is a perfectly logical reason for being overweight. For example a client said: "I've got a pony to look after" she was blaming a pony for giving her stress to wrongly justify self-abuse. Looking after a pony is good exercise, even though she didn't see the situation in a positive light due to her warped sense of reality, which of course is caused by being depressed due to being overweight.

Some clients will say: "I don't make excuses or blame others." But this is in itself an excuse, because of course they make excuses and blame others or they would not be overweight. If they truly blamed them self for their weight problem, then neurological pain would be associated to over eating, preventing them from eating wrongly and so they would be slim. Hence the fact that they do blame others, and they make excuses, regardless of the client's denial of this. For example: a client told me that she blames no one but herself and she never makes excuses. She was adamant with this claim and so I had to prove to her that she was wrong. In order to avoid conflict I simply waited for her to contradict herself and it emerged that she would go and buy crisps for herself and husband, he had one flavour and she had another, but yet she would eat hers and his flavoured crisp. So unknown to this client, she was blaming her husband for buying so many crisps with the delusional idea of the other flavour being off limits to her, because they were her husband's, but yet she still ate them. So her husband was her excuse for buying and eating more crisps, she would say to herself when buying: "These are not mine, they are my husband's." That took away her guilt of buying and eating them, hence the husband being her excuse. She was unknowingly blaming him for eating so many crisps and gaining the weight.

This same client told me that she drank five bottles of wine a week because she was always socialising with friends. In other words she was blaming her friends for her drinking problem that was putting weight onto her. It emerged that she would drink everyday regardless of whether her friends where there or not, so she was using her friends as an excuse to drink, even when alone. Due to her dependence on alcohol each day that she was using in order to disassociate herself from the reality of her life, she was clearly an alcoholic in denial. She was shocked when I explained to her that she was an alcoholic and this created an abreaction for the greater good. She accepted that I was right about her blaming others and her alcoholism; this was a revelation for her and the same goes for all clients, once they hear the truth about themselves. You can class this as a shock tactic from me, the therapist, and due to being truthful and direct to the clients, they all appreciate the honesty, and it is what is needed for clients that self-harm.

Another weight loss client said to me: "I have two cans of larger a night because it's my signal that the day has ended and I can then relax."

I delved deeper into this and she had recently been to India were they do not allow the drinking of alcohol, and she said: "I knew the drink wasn't there" and knowing no alcohol was there caused her anxiety. This client was unknowingly gaining weight due to being an alcoholic. She was shocked when I told her that she was an alcoholic and she said: "Well I'm not over drinking because its only two cans a night." I explained that she had become dependent on the drink due to it bothering her when it was not there on holiday. So at what point is a person an alcoholic or not? Whether they have six or two cans a night is irrelevant, the person is still dependent on it and therefore is an alcoholic, because it is no longer a social past time, it's seven days a week of drinking. Once that was explained to her she agreed that she was an alcoholic and that she had turned to drink as a comfort after her brother's suicide some ten years previous to the session with me. Remember cause and effect, the brothers death was the cause of depression and the drink the added effect as a deluded comfort. She had been an alcoholic for ten years and at no point had she realised that fact. The reason she drank no more than two cans was because her children needed looking after by her because she was a single mum. I explained that in the past she had turned to drink as a comfort because she did not want to deal with the loss of her brother, and she was also using drink to mask her depression of feeling lonely as a single mum. I asked: "What is going to happen when your children grow up and leave home, and you are living alone with nothing to occupy you? You will get more depressed and turn to drink more because the children are no longer there to occupy you, so this has to stop today." Notice how I answered the question for the client as my way of leading her to abreact, so that I could associate the pain to drinking alcohol within her mind. Of course I compounded the fear later in the session whilst the client was in trance and by using timeline I made her witness a devastating future having never met me. No one wants to live with an alcoholic, so in order to find a partner she again needed to stop drinking alcohol. The fear of the future negative event of drinking more, being more overweight and being alone, created fear within her mind and that associated pain I reassociated to the thought of drinking alcohol (anchor), so therefore she stopped drinking, lost weight and is healthier with the added benefit of being happier. Obviously I ended the session on a positive note of finding love and showing this client a positive future event without the drink and I gave her mind permission to grieve, which she had previously been suppressing, so she was able to move forwards in life.

Now and then you will get a very challenging client that is so convinced they do not over eat junk because they are sure that they only eat healthy foods. They will talk for over an hour telling you all the fruit and vegetables they eat, and small meals. They will tell you: "I don't snack that often and it was over a week ago since I had a chocolate bar." Other than a serious medical condition, the only other reasons this client is overweight is that she eats large amounts of the wrong foods, or she drinks sugary liquids. This type of weight loss client is in total denial and they have convinced themselves that they are a responsible eater. You need to allow more time in the session for this type of challenging client. After an hour or so, they will start to tell you the truth, due to the use of the skills I have taught you. Yes, it was over a week ago since she had a chocolate bar, but conveniently for her she forgot to tell me that the night after, she had a packet of biscuits, next night cheese crackers, and the next night crisps and so on. It then emerges that the reason she has small meals is because she spread the meals out throughout the course of the whole day. In other words she was constantly snacking and that is why the main meals are small.

These challenging clients are not intending to lie to me, they just were not aware that they were in such denial.

One client said: "I always leave food on my plate and that was good because it means I was not overeating." Of course I knew this was an excuse but I needed to delve deeper. It turns out that as an adult she would leave food on her plate as a way of rebelling against her dad, because as a child he made her eat every bite, even if she did not want it. Therefore now, as an adult, in order to compensate for the food she was now leaving, she would cook too much food and over fill her plate, so she was still overeating. She no longer lived with her dad but yet the childlike mentality of rebelling against him was still within her. This of course was due to the age of the associated link being that of a child within her subconscious, with the anchor being meal time and the associated emotion being that of a child rebelling against the authority of her dad. Once she was aware of this fact, she saw how daft the situation was, and it never happened again and as a result she lost weight.

Another client said to me: "The other day I had a cake, so I thought, well I've ruined my day's diet, so might as well have another." This client was placing her guilt onto the cake as if it was the cakes fault and not hers for her own self-abuse. Another client said: "I had cereal at 3pm; I've blown being slim for the day, so fuck it." Clearly this client was depressed and angry at herself for the self-abuse, so she then comfort eats, as a deluded, short term fix, which then creates more depression and the self-abuse cycle starts again until stopped in therapy.

Out of all the many excuses I have heard over the years, this one amazed me the most. This was a male client and he told me: "The reason I am overweight is because I have a genetic disorder." I asked him: "Have you been told this by your doctor, after having a test?" He replied: "No." Considering he had no medical proof, it was obvious that I had to ridicule this excuse of a genetic disorder and make the client aware of how ridiculous the imagined thought was. Even so, it is important that I go about this slowly so as not to cause confrontation, I needed the client to think for himself, so I led him to realise how daft his thought process was. I asked him: "Are your children overweight?" And again, he said: "No." In fact, his two teenage boys were very fit, due to being into sports and both were slim. I made the point of telling him: "Surely if you had a genetic disorder you would have passed it on to your sons." He looked confused and after some thought he told me that I had a good point. I then asked him: "Do your parents have a genetic disorder that makes them overweight?" He said: "I don't know." His answer surprised me and confused me for a little while, because how could he not know whether his parents were overweight or not. To my amazement, he told me that he had never met any of his blood relatives because he was adopted. So, how can he possibly think he had a genetic disorder? This was another client that was in total denial of overeating. To block out his guilt of self-abuse, he had fantasised about having this medical condition, therefore he was blaming an imagined, genetic illness for his weight problem, instead of himself.

Dear student, in this client's mind there is something else at work that he is not consciously aware of, and it is to do with the main reason he imagined a genetic illness, that he later used as an excuse to overeat. Can you think of what the main reason is? Take a moment to think before reading on.

He was manifesting this genetic disorder as a way of making an imagined, psychological connection with his biological parents that he had never met, due to having no real contact with them. He had done that because it helped him cope with his sense of abandonment as a baby from his real genetic parents, when they placed him in foster care. The imagined, genetic illness gave him a comforting connection to his real parents, so clearly he longed for a real connection. Again this is the cause and effect, the abandonment being the true cause of depression and the effect being overeating, which created weight gain and health problems. Another fascinating case I'm sure you will agree.

Many weight loss clients will hide chocolate, or other foods in their own home that they know are wrong for them, and then hours later they act out the scenario that they just happen to stumble upon these junk foods. They ask themselves who could have put that there, and it would be such a shame to throw it out, so they eat it all. Some clients will even hide food at their parent's home, even though they don't live their parents, and later they convince themselves that their mother bought it for them as a weekend treat.

Yes, dear student that has genuinely happened with some of my weight loss clients and again, these clients must be shown how ridiculous this is. Again, please note that you are ridiculing the situation and not the person.

I have had many clients hide toffee wrappers in the car, and at the bottom of bins, so that their partner could not see the wrappers. What does a child do when they have been naughty? They hide the evidence and make excuses to mummy and daddy saying: "It's not me, it's someone else's fault, and I didn't do it". This is again a childlike mentality due to the age of the associated link. What does a weight loss client do when they have been naughty by binge eating? They make excuses just like a child, but instead of making it to mummy and daddy, they make it to themselves. So where their weight is concerned, the client is acting like a child, however this does not mean they are childish in all aspects of life, it just means where their weight is concerned, they are very childlike. Well, it is time they started being the adult that they are, where eating the wrong foods are concerned, they must be told that and educated on the mind model. All clients will agree that their thought processes are childlike, once you have pointed out their excuses, lies, and all are grateful to be told. Do not think this is insulting to the clients, because it is not, as they are thankful for the truth and honesty. Simply tell them: "I am telling you this to give you a reality check and by doing so we are saving your life today and the quality of your future happiness, and health in life."

Another client said: "When I get home from work I don't have time to cook a meal so I have to order a take-away." A large number of clients will tell themselves that same excuse via habitual speech or thought. I make it known to the client that they think they do not have time to cook a ten minute meal, but yet they have time to sit there for an hour waiting for the take-away. They then, once again, realise how ridiculous that excuse was, and therefore they cannot use it again. So, in the future they will spend ten minutes cooking a healthy meal because it takes less time than waiting for junk to arrive.

"I don't know when I'm full," again, another ridiculous excuse. I make it known to the client that their body has sent them the signal that they are satisfied with the amount of food they have eaten, but yet they ignored the signal so their body and mind becomes confused and therefore no longer knows what the feeling of having enough food is, because the signal was ignored and they kept eating. So the client must retrain the mind and body into knowing what a satisfied feeling is. This is explained in more detail later.

"I didn't eat the chocolate all at once; I only ate half, and had the other half later." The client said the above, but ate both halves of the chocolate within a half hour, but by cutting it in half. Kidology was at work as yet another ridiculous excuse to deny that the whole chocolate bar was eaten. A client on the phone to me before booking a session said: "It's not going to be easy to lose weight". In their mind the excuses had already begun, however I quickly turned their sentence around by saying: "The last part of what you said is right because it is easy to lose weight." Another example. A man and his wife were in a joint session with me, even though I rarely conduct a session for two people at once, even so, I agreed to do so because they felt that together would be more beneficial for them. The man could not understand why he was putting weight on, and so in this instant it was good to have his wife in the session as well, because she knew things that he was not telling me, which made my job easy. For instance: she went out for the day, and when she got back half a tub of butter was missing from a newly opened tub that she had placed in the fridge. He had unknowingly eaten half a tub of butter on toast with jam. Of course he knew he was eating toast but not how much he had consumed. This is a classic sign of a subconscious eater and I will explain this in detail later. Basically he consciously did not know how many pieces of toast he had consumed, so he did not know the amount of butter he had eaten. Just think how much fat he was consuming from half a tub of butter.

Dear student, all the excuses cannot be made to look silly, because you will find out from experience that many clients have been abused as a child or adult in some way. The victim of abuse then abuses them self with foods as comfort and becomes fat, with the wrong warped thought that they are punishing the person that once abused them, because the abuser no longer has control over them. Therefore the self-abuse is giving the victim a deluded sense of control over their own life that was once out of control due to being controlled by an abuser. Basically the victim thinks they have taken back control of their life but they have gone about it wrongly due to their warped sense of reality. Of course that is a childlike mentality with the thought of, look at me, I can now do what I want and you can't stop me by controlling me, which hurts you. The victim also wrongly thinks that by making themselves fat, no one will look at them in a sexual way again, so no one will abuse them again and therefore they have associated pleasure to overeating, plus the pleasurable thought of the warped sense of control, when in fact they are out of control, because now they are depressed over being fat. The original abuse was the cause, the overeating the effect for comfort and a sense of control, and being fat was a secondary effect that leads to more depression. This type of client must learn to understand that the abuser in the past does not care whether they are fat or not, they are not the ones suffering. This type of client must be told that the only person suffering now is them and it is now self-inflicted abuse. They have become the abuser of them self. The past is the past, and it cannot be changed, even so, their perception of it can change. Instead of punishing themselves they must be told to prove the world wrong, ego boost and confidence boost the client. Make them feel wanted in the world, make them see how many friends and loved ones they have etc, and despite the past, they have still achieved a good job, or whatever it may be. Make these abused clients see a better, fitter life and make them aware that with them being happy, fit and healthy will hurt their past abuser, unlike what they have been doing to them self.

One client told me: "Something drastic has to happen to my health before I start to look after myself." Of course, by then it would be too late, so she needed to be aware of this. In the hypnosis part of the session I made her see a negative future event, as if she had never met me, and therefore she would have continued with all her excuses to over eat. It is very important that you make the client realise that this future negative event is only happening as if they had never met you, the hypnotherapist. You would not want them to walk away thinking that negative future is what is going to happen, now that they have met you, this is very important and I have mentioned that a number of times in the book. In this future event, I made her see herself having ill health due to being overweight, and the loss of the quality of life she would have had. This was obviously upsetting for her and therefore the positive affect and an abreaction occurred, which I then associated all that emotion to the anchor of overeating. After making her see this event, it is once again so very important that you make the client realise that you have met today, and that event will never happen, as their health improves by changing their lifestyle, so the client is then shown a positive future away from over eating. She was so grateful after the session, that I had saved her from that devastating future event, that the following week she phoned me to thank me again. She had lost some weight, and no longer did she need something drastic to happen to her health in real life in order to start looking after herself. This of course was because I had shown her under hypnosis a drastic event that she now wanted to avoid. Simply put, I associated pain to self-abuse and pleasure to not self-abusing.

A large number of clients will binge eat, and then keep themselves occupied later, as a way of disassociating themselves from the negative abuse they have just done. This is self-denial and kidology at work again. As with the last true example, this type of client must see the devastating future events that will occur if they continue this denial. Also a large number of weight loss clients will see themselves wrongly, as being slim when they look in a mirror. That is because they have created their own reality to suit their denial. What is reality is explained in the volume one book, so to understand this more, please read the reality chapter again.

In short, reality is not what we see; it is what is created within our own minds, it is an individual's perception, be it real or imagined and therefore it is still their reality. This must be explained to the client and that their warped reality will damage their future life. One client said to me: "I have a magic mirror at home that I can look into and I look slim," this client was not joking; she genuinely believed it due to her warped sense of reality as a coping mechanism to suppress her true situation.

Apart from hypnosis, there is only one other way to get clients to see themselves as they really look, and that is to take a photo of them. Advise clients to go home and take a picture selfie and place it on the fridge, or cake tin, and look at it every day as a reminder of why they must lose weight. I took a photo of one client and she was happy with that, until I asked her: "Do you want to look at it?" She then started to scream, placed her hands over her face, and she went into the foetal position, as if reverting back to being a baby. She was horrified at the thought of seeing her true self, and she had no self-worth due to lack of confidence. This extreme type of client may take two sessions or more, but this is very rare.

One client told me that she went to Weight Watchers meetings every Wednesday evening, but it was not helping at all and she could not understand why. Once there, she would be weighed, and after the meeting she would go home and binge eat every Wednesday night, she told me. Her justification for this binge eating was that her weight loss week did not start until Thursday morning of every week because she would not be weighed again until the Wednesday evening after. So even though she had told me that, she had still not made the connection within her mind that the binge eating was the reason why at Weight Watchers she had lost no weight. Once again, you can see how destructive and silly this way of thinking is, but until told, the client is not aware of that fact. Clients genuinely believe that their way of thinking is universal, that everyone thinks the same, so it is totally normal. They have no concept that what they say are ridiculous excuses and not rational at all until told.

I was walking through a supermarket, when I paused at the chocolate aisle to watch two overweight women, they were several feet away from one another, picking up different chocolate bars and looking at them. I could see the guilt on their faces as they did this, when suddenly, one got all excited, smiling, jumping in the air and shouted to the other woman: "Oh look, this one is low fat." At that point they both started to grab several of those bars each, to buy. They used the low fat content as an excuse to buy and eat more bars than normal, it took away their guilt. They might as well be eating full fat bars, in smaller numbers. So, in short, people that are overweight blame everyone and everything else for their problem, apart from themselves, by making up excuses, regardless of their denial of that fact. It is the partner's fault, because he/she wants chocolate when in fact, they do not. It's the kid's fault, they stress me out, it's works fault, it's the fault of that wedding I have to go to, I'm addicted, or they are simply in total denial of what they are doing.

Dear student, what follows is the pre-talk to the hypnotic induction that you can say to the client. I have written both the pre-talk and what is said under hypnosis far longer than need be. I have done this purposely to give you more examples of what can be said; so that you can pick and choose what you may feel fits that particular client best. So, in short, this script is not intended to be read word for word to the weight loss client. It can even be used in a number of sessions if needed, to make them different from the previous. With weight loss, if you are ever in doubt, do not continue with the session. For instance, I had a very attractive, slim young woman for a weight loss session. Of course she did not need a session for weight loss, but not to add negativity and disappointment within her mind, I did not tell her this at first. I did a session on boosting her confidence and explained to her later that it is what she needed, and not a weight loss session, she was happy with the outcome.

Start here, Weight Loss Pre-talk

What follows is the Pre-talk to the hypnotic induction. I have written both the pre-talk and what is said under hypnosis, far longer than it needs be. I have done this purposely, to give you more examples of what can be said and so that you can pick and choose what you may feel fits that particular client best. So, in short, this script is not intended to be read word for word to the client. It can even be used in a number of sessions if needed, to make them different from the previous, and please remember to always personalise a session to the client.

I always start by asking the client about their problem and situation to gain the information needed for the session. This time also allows me the time needed to build rapport. I then ask: "Do you agree that there are two parts of the human mind, the conscious mind (their conscious will) and the subconscious mind (their imagination)?" All would tend to agree with that there are two parts.

Dear student please note, I never mention the third part of the mind, the analytical area of the mind to a client, because they do not need that information. So keep it simple. I only gave that information to you because you are my student, and of course, you are not training a student, they are a client, so the two parts of the mind is all they need to know.

I then ask the client: "Which part of the mind is in control of what you will be doing day-to-day?" And 99% of the time, clients will say: "The conscious mind." This is for two reasons: firstly, most people think they are consciously in control, and secondly, I also lead the client in the direction of saying: "Conscious Mind."

Dear student, how do I lead a client to say: "Conscious mind and why"? Think about that question, because the answer you have already been taught and therefore you know, even if you think you don't know.

This is what I do. I ask: "Do you agree that there are two parts of the mind, the conscious mind and the subconscious mind?" When I say: "Conscious mind," I lift my left hand, and by doing so I have created an anchor within the client's mind of the thought of: "Conscious Mind" being associated to my left hand, which is the anchor. I then put my left hand down and then when saying: "Subconscious Mind," I raise my right hand, and therefore by doing so I have created an anchor (right hand) associated to the words and thought of the: "Subconscious Mind" and then I put my right hand down. I then ask the client: "Which part of the mind is in control of what you will be doing day-to-day?" At the same time of asking that question, I reactivate the anchor with the association of thinking of the: "Conscious Mind" by simply raising my left hand, and so the client is led to answer the question by saying: "Conscious Mind" and then I put my left hand down. I then tell the client: "You are in fact wrong. It is the subconscious mind (reinforce the anchor by raising the right hand) that is in control and I will explain why later in the session" (then drop the right hand). I then reassure them that everyone gets it wrong and that avoids any confrontation and prevents the client from feeling foolish.

Dear student, can you think of why I have done that? Why had I led the client to think and say: "Conscious Mind" when it is wrong? How do I benefit from this as a therapist? Well I benefit in five ways as follows:

First benefit, I now know the client can be led, and therefore they are suggestible, which makes the session easy.

Second benefit, I also created a third anchor, can you work out what the third anchor is? It is not an obvious one, so I wouldn't expect even an experience therapist to figure out what I have done. I'll give you a hint. The first anchor was my left hand associated to thinking of and therefore saying the: "Conscious Mind." The second anchor was my right hand associated to the thought of the: "Subconscious Mind" and the third anchor was created once I said: "You are in fact wrong, it is the subconscious mind." It was at this point that the third anchor was created when I reinforced the second anchor by raising the right hand.

Even though I have given you that information, I still wouldn't expect you to have worked out what the third anchor is or what it is for, if you have, then well done you. When I lifted my right hand a second time I was reinforcing the second anchor to the thought of the subconscious mind. However because at that point I had made the client aware that the subconscious was the right answer, I had also then quickly changed the second anchor (right hand) to now thinking it's right (correct answer). So now the second anchor's association has been changed from thinking of the subconscious mind to realising it is right, it is the correct answer. Once the new association to the anchor (right hand) was created, I put my right hand down, so that the associated link to being right remained to be used again later in the session.

So I can class this as a new second anchor or third anchor with the original association to the second anchor having now been replaced. Remember the subconscious can only ever remember the last thing that was associated to an anchor. In this case the new thought of knowing it is right (correct answer) to the anchor of the right hand. The original association to the second anchor was: "Subconscious Mind" but that association had served its purpose and was no longer needed, so I replaced it for the added benefit of leading the client to associate the right hand to represent the right answer, the correct answer, which implies the right thing to do. I can use this anchor later in the session when I want to provoke, or lead the client to the right answer to whatever future question I ask them. Notice that I use the right hand for the right answer and not the left, hence why: "Conscious Mind" association was left hand, as it was the wrong answer. If I had made the right hand as the anchor for the wrong answer, then it would not have had the same use, and it would have been confusing for the client due to the word: "Right" hand being used for wrong and not right. Always use right hand anchor for a leading signal for the right answer or right thing to do, as in my opinion it should be. I will be using this signal anchor later in the script.

Third benefit of leading the client to say: "Conscious Mind" is the creation of a "Trans-Derivational Search (TDS)" within their mind by me replying with saying: "You are in fact wrong, it is the subconscious mind that is in control and I will explain why later in the session." By saying that I created a: "Trans-Derivational Search (TDS)" within the client's mind because they are now consciously wondering how could they be wrong. How can it be the subconscious that is in control, and I wonder how he is going to explain this? This sent the conscious mind on a journey and therefore bypassed via TDS, which opens up their subconscious to suggestion, which cements the anchor of right hand meaning right answer, the right thing to do.

Fourth benefit is that the client's subconscious knows I am in control. When a client is led to answer wrongly, they accept that they were wrong because I proved to them, with my knowledge that I am right. The client knows that I am right, and so they will agree to all future suggestions and commands from me as being right. I have become the authority figure of reason, truth and knowing what is right. My knowledge gains the clients trust in me. This way I avoid confrontation within the session because the client knows I must be right throughout, regardless of any opposing ideas they may have previously had.

Fifth benefit is that the client is now in light trance due to the TDS and rapport built.

I continue by asking for information about the client, that way I can personalise the session to suit them. What have they tried in the past? What their routine is at the moment? I personalise the pre-talk based on the information the client provides.

I ask questions like:

1) Why are you here today?
2) How much food do you eat on average?
3) Tell me about your daily routine?
4) What is your goal weight?
5) Why do you want to lose weight now?
6) What is the most important reason for you losing weight? This may sound obvious, but it is important to get you to focus on your reasons.
7) What excuses do you make to yourself? (Most say none until you tell them later in the session the examples from other clients that they then can relate to, or wait until they make excuses to feed it back to them when needed).
8) Do you find you eat more in certain circumstances?
9) Tell me about a happy time in your life? But if you cannot think of one straightaway, then imagine a time when you would feel happy.
10) What is your fear in relation to your weight?

The information gathered from these questions can be used later in the session. The more information I have on their problem, the more successful the session will be.

For instance, if their reason for losing weight was for their children's sake, or their own health, I would ask for more information on this and therefore the session becomes more personal to them.

I continue the pre-talk by telling my clients: "Personalised sessions are far more successful than a group session. That is why I do not do group sessions, because each individual is different, and you are the only person that matters at the moment." (By saying that makes the client feel important and of course they are).

Three Different Types of Eaters

This is said to the client: "Did you know that there are three different types of eaters? And I need to know the type you are. You could be a mixture of all three, two, or just one, however most people are all three. In order to deal with your weight problem you need to understand the problem more."

1) **Emotional Eaters** - Emotional eaters are people who eat food because of emotions such as stress, worry, loneliness, boredom, frustration, companionship, reward, punishment, or any other emotion that is manifested in eating. This type of eater is also called a Comfort Eater.

2) **Conditioned Eaters** - A conditioned eater is a person who overeats due to conditioning from early childhood, such as the child that was made to feel guilty if they left anything on their plate because the parents told them: "People are starving in other countries so be grateful for the food and eat it." Please note that even though most conditioned eaters develop from childhood, a conditioned eating can also be conditioned in adulthood, for example: from a controlling partner. A conditioned eater can also be a person that, when they were a child, they were motivated to eat everything on their plate in order to get dessert. So, pleasure has been associated to eating all the foods that are in front of them, and a feeling of guilt to not eating the food. Also a sweet toothed eater can develop by conditioning in childhood, for example: when a child is upset, or has been good, the adult gives sweets and the child grows up thinking that junk foods are a reward, due to the associated conditioning. So, later in life, they still wrongly feel rewarded by eating junk and this has the negative effect of obesity. Another way a person can become a conditioned eater is if they have been cooking for a family of four for years, then the children grow up, and move out of the family home, but the cook continues with cooking the same amount of food for four people, even though only two remaining people live in the house, so the two remaining people are eating two meals each instead of one each. They do not know they are doing this until told.

3) **Subconscious Eaters** - A subconscious eater is a person who is unaware of all the food that they are putting into their mouths, for example: watching a movie and eating a whole bag of popcorn or a tub of ice cream. This type of eater is continuously snacking at work, at the sweet basket on the table or desk, and is not aware of how much they are eating throughout the day. A subconscious eater is an automatic eater and is not aware of their overeating habit.

These three types of eaters tend to be connected, for example: every time a child is upset the parents gave the child sweets to comfort them. So, as the child grows up the person has it conditioned into them, by the parents, to associate sweets as comfort, then as an adult every time the person is upset they reach for the chocolate or foods that they know are wrong for them because it has become a conditioned habit of feeling emotional pleasure with eating food, hence the emotional eater from associated conditioning. The conditioning became repetitious so the subconscious took overeating on as a habit, hence a subconscious eater, so every time the person feels depressed they subconsciously eat out of an emotionally (comfort) conditioned need.

Until that is explained to the client, they genuinely do not know why they became overweight, or why they are overeating. I will give you an example of conditioned subconscious eaters. Take two tables with ten people on. Each person is the same weight, height, and age. Both tables are given identical bowls of chicken legs, same weight, number etc. Table "A" – every time they eat a chicken leg, they put the leftover bone on a plate in front of them. Table "B" – every time they eat a chicken leg, the waiter comes and removes the leftover bone. In the end, the people on table "B" eat 50% more chicken legs than table "A." The reason being is that table "B" did not have a representation of the number of chicken legs they had eaten. Alternatively the people on table "A" could see the leftover bones and think to them self: "Well I've had four, that's enough for me." This prevented the people on table "A" from overeating. So it is very important to remember how much food has been eaten in order to know when to stop eating.

Weight Loss Mind Model

The following is said to the client. "The mind is split up into two parts; you have got the conscious and the subconscious parts of the mind. At the beginning of this session you thought that you were consciously in control of your life, however as we continue you will realise that the conscious is the part of the mind that we would like to think is in control, but it is not, it is the subconscious mind that is in control.

For example: you do not think about breathing, blood circulation, making your heart beat, because the subconscious is the auto pilot for the body, it is running the body twenty four hours a day, seven days a week. This part of the mind can do many things at a time and whilst it is running the body, it is also taking in two million pieces of information every second, passing on what it thinks is important to the conscious mind and disregarding the rest. For example: you buy a new car and you are driving down the road in your new car, and now it seems like every other car is the same as yours, they are even the same colour. Even though you cannot remember seeing so many of these same cars the day before, so did everyone go and buy the identical type of new car at the same time as you? No, of course not, it is just the day before the subconscious noticed all these cars, but it thought that type of car was not important to you, so did not pass the information on to the conscious mind. Therefore you were not fully aware of them even though they were there and you saw them. But now you have this new car, it has got to be important to you because you first imagined buying and driving the car and then you consciously did what you had previously imagined. Because in order to do anything in life, we have first got to imagine doing it, so because you imagined it and then did it, the subconscious realises this car is now important to you and so now it passes the information on every time it sees this type of car, so you are now consciously aware of seeing more of those cars than you have ever seen in your life. You see the two parts of the mind have become friends where the thought of this car is concerned.

That is what you have not done with your weight problem, you have never imagined yourself slim so there is still conflict with the conscious and subconscious mind and when the will (conscious) and imagination (subconscious) are in conflict, the imagination always wins, due to the subconscious being the more powerful part of the whole mind. You see you have made a conscious decision to lose weight, but you have not been able to, because you tried to solve your problem on a conscious level, but your problem is within your subconscious mind, let me explain.

The conscious part of the mind is very logical and very rational; it is the part that you use when making your decisions on a day-to-day basis, but it is the imagination (subconscious) that determines on whether we carry out those conscious decisions or not. Last week you may have made the conscious decision to go swimming, but then you imagined that the water was cold. How do you know? You did not go swimming because this imagined negative thought of the water being cold stopped you doing something in which you had made a conscious decision to do. Therefore your subconscious mind is in control. This is what has happened with your weight (other bad habit) problem. You consciously want to lose weight (stop the bad habit) but you are playing a different movie within your subconscious imagination, again conflict is at work, so you will never lose weight when only trying consciously. The conscious mind is the part where your willpower is held, but of course, you have got to remember to use it. I know you can use it because you had the will to get up this morning, wash and clothe yourself, so we know it is there.

The conscious part of your mind can think of only one thought or idea at once, this is why we can only concentrate on doing one task at a time when doing it consciously, although, we can still do many tasks at once, but only one is conscious and the others are subconscious in the form of a habit, be it a good or bad habit. The conscious mind is a very a slow part of the mind, and this is why we get stressed out, we try to do too many things at the same time consciously and our minds cannot do it. You know what happens, the phone rings, the children want your attention and you are trying to cook the evening meal, you are stressed out because you are trying to do all three tasks at once. Take a step back, realise what is happening and do one task at a time. Doing one task does not get us stressed; trying to do two tasks consciously starts the stress ball rolling. It is like a snowball rolling down a hill, the more tasks you try to do at once the more the stress builds up, and once we get stressed out, we are then not able to do any of the tasks we were trying to do. Stop, take a step back in your mind, realise what is happening and why you are stressed and do just one task at a time to remove or limit the stress. Due to the stress build up described, you then needed comforting, due to the negative emotion, and you started snacking, overeating etc. The first time this happened, you consciously put the food to your mouth, and had a bite. You probably felt guilty, but you kept going as a deluded comfort, which can be for emotional or conditioned reasons. Then over time, several cakes, snacks, take-aways later, the subconscious part of the mind said: I can do that job for you and it took it on as a habit to free up your conscious mind's burden, so your subconscious thinks it is doing you a favour. Because all a habit is, is something you do consciously a number of times and then the subconscious will take it on as a habit. The subconscious part of the mind knows that you can only consciously concentrate on doing one task at a time, so the more jobs the subconscious can do on your behalf the better. So as far as the subconscious is concerned, it is doing you a favour by taking on the problem as a habit because also the subconscious does not know it is a problem, it is just a habit that you want to do as far as your subconscious is concerned and it will keep the habit until you subconsciously remove the habit by changing the positive associated link to a negative one, so that you avoid the bad habit, and we will do that via hypnosis later. Driving is another habit, again when you first started to learn to drive you drove consciously, you had to think about mirror, signal, brakes, clutch and what is going on around you, it was cognitively exhausting due to being conscious thought. It was impossible to have a conversation or think about what you did the day before or what to do later in the day, again due to the conscious mind only being able to do one task at once and that was driving. But later, over time, you passed your test and practised and so now you do not even need to think about how to drive. You are driving down the road and someone pulls out in front of you and you just stop, you did not have to consciously think about stopping, it happened subconsciously. When you drive home from work, before you know it, you are home and cannot consciously remember the details of most of the journey you have just had, even though you know the journey you have taken because you take the same route every day, so your subconscious has taken it on as a habit, so you subconsciously drove home. That is called: "Highway Hypnosis" because you are no longer consciously driving and that is why you can now have a conversation when driving and you can think of other thoughts. Your life is full of habits. Swimming is a habit, riding a bike, reading, walking, the way you brush your teeth in the morning, because you no longer need to give it any conscious thought, they are all now subconscious actions.

Our lives are full of habits because all habits are created by something you first did consciously a number of times that is then taken on by the subconscious as a habit. Now at the moment the subconscious is protecting these habits, it does not want you to forget to drive as you drive down the road, it does not want you forget how to swim whilst swimming across a river. It is also protecting the habit of overeating (or whatever the bad habit is) because the subconscious does not know the difference between a good or bad habit; a habit is a habit as far as the subconscious is concerned, so it is still playing the old memory for why you wanted to snack or over eat in the first place. It is still running the memory of something that your subconscious still thinks you want to do, so you are fighting between the two parts of your mind. The conscious knows all the reasons why you want to lose weight, but the subconscious is still rerunning the old reasons for why you started snacking or overeating in the first place. That is why when you try and give up by using willpower alone, the conscious mind gets the cravings, because you say to yourself, right, I am not going to eat that junk in the evening.

Now the evening comes along and the subconscious knows you always had junk in the evening, so when you do not have junk it sets off an alarm in your head to remind you, which makes you feel anxious until you once again carry out the bad habit. If you still do not have food in your mouth it starts to produce cravings and desires, because the subconscious is reminding you to do something that it thinks you still want to do, it is reminding you of the habit. You have seen this craving as a negative thing and given into it, in a delusional attempt to feel better. But this craving is a positive thing because it means you have won by not eating the cake or junk foods in that moment. This is where the habit of eating junk food then becomes an associated link, let me explain.

The subconscious holds all your memories, you have got memories stored within your subconscious going all the way back to childhood, but you cannot consciously always recall them, but then a song might come on the radio and all of a sudden you can remember a memory that you have associated to that song, who you were with, what you were doing, even what you were wearing in that past time and the emotions you felt. You see the human mind works by association, when we experience two things together for a little while, one will automatically remind us of the other in the future. So, for example: when you are in a situation that is depressing, boring, or stressful, you turn to food as a deluded comfort. You have created a habit, then you have associated stress to certain situations signalling to your subconscious mind to make you eat through emotional, habit conditioned reasons, as if the subconscious is doing you a favour to comfort you, when in fact the habit is destroying your health and quality of life. Also in the subconscious are all your emotions, for example: you do not think, I have been in a good mood for the last seven days; I am going to make a conscious decision to wake up in a bad mood tomorrow. All your emotions are controlled by the subconscious.

So, due to the habit, you eat subconsciously once that negative emotional association has been triggered via there activated anchor of stress, depression whatever the anchor may be. By doing so this gives you a delusional sense of pleasure, but then later guilt sets in and you are back where you started, feeling stressed and putting on more weight, which stresses and damages your body even more. Over time you have created many associated links towards eating junk food, for example: walking into the kitchen reactivates a signal within your subconscious to open the fridge, or biscuit tin, and nibble at whatever is there. (For example: getting in the car and lighting up.) Because this habit formed associated link is in the subconscious mind, you subconsciously eat without consciously knowing how much food you have consumed. To consciously attempt to give into this powerful associated link, that your mind's subconscious created through a habit, would be impossible. You have got to do it on a subconscious level through the imagination, because that is where the problem is. It is the associated link that we need to change later in the session by making a new negative associated link to replace the old positive one of eating junk, and also we need to change the association to a positive one of not eating junk. Also where you once associated doing the bad habit, we need to change the association to the anchor of doing something else in that same place instead of self-abuse. The reason you have not been able to lose weight is because your imagination is in the subconscious and the imagination is very powerful. For example: you have probably had dreams or nightmares before and you have woken up shaking, sweating and your heart pounding, but yet you have not been anywhere, you are still in bed. Well this is because the subconscious part of the mind does not know the difference between something real or imagined, both are your reality. So if you are having this dream of running down the road scared, as far as the subconscious is concerned it is actually happening, therefore it makes physical changes to the body, hence you wake up shaking, sweating and your heart pounding. So that is what you do in a session with me, you use the imagination under hypnosis, because if you imagine that it is going to be easy to lose weight, then you are right, but if you imagine it is going to be difficult you are also right. You see if you imagine it is going to be easy to lose the weight then your subconscious will make it easy for you.

The problem is that in the past a lot of the time when you tried to stop overeating or cut out junk food, you are consciously saying to yourself: "I will not eat that cake" or crisps or whatever it may be. Well, what are you imagining when you say that? Yes that is right, you are imagining eating that cake, so you are getting the subconscious to imagine eating food that you know is wrong for you and that is making it difficult for you to stop because you have implanted a powerful suggestion of eating the cake, you then eat the cake. This is because when the will (conscious) and imagination (subconscious) are in conflict, the imagination will always win because it is the more powerful part of the mind. For example: if you consciously think, do not think of a black cat, you have then imagined a black cat, making it impossible to stop imagining the cat. What you consciously wanted to achieve "Do not think of a black cat" has had the opposite effect on the subconscious mind and this thought is acted upon just the same as consciously thinking I don't want that cake. You have gone about your weight problem consciously and it has had the opposite effect, don't think of eating a cake consciously, so you subconscious imagines eating it and therefore do so.

Now what you have got to do is imagine it is going to be easy for you to stop overeating or binge eating junk food, you need to imagine not eating a cake instead of imagining eating it. You have, as I have mentioned, got associations with certain activities and eating the wrong foods, for example: first thing in the morning or whilst driving, and certain times when you regularly snack. Now imagine those situations without the snacks, which is what you need to do, for example: if you have snacks or overeat in the evening, you can imagine that morning that you are going to have an evening without the snacks and eating fruit instead.

Because you have imagined doing that, without having snacks, when the evening comes your subconscious just makes it easy for you not to snack. Because you have already imagined what is going to happen, that you were not snacking at that time, so the habit formed associated link is broken and the subconscious remembers the new healthier habit link of eating fruit for example. You see you have been telling yourself on a conscious level that you want to stop gaining weight, and lose weight, but you have not been able to because your weight problem is within the subconscious mind, even though you are consciously aware of it, you have never told the subconscious it is time to change, the emotional, subconscious and conditioned eating problem. You have been going about your weight problem all wrong, and that is where I come in, to help you on a subconscious level through hypnosis.

So this is where hypnosis comes in, there is no magic trick or waving of a magic wand with hypnosis, it is a way of getting you to relax, and because you are relaxed I can talk directly to your subconscious, the part that is in control. Because I am talking to the subconscious, together we can rerecord an up-to-date memory that snacking etc, is bad for you and it is something you do not want to do. So we are taking away the old memory and replacing it with the new memory of not wanting to overeat. Now there is no need for cravings and desires because you have both parts of the mind working as one to keep you from gaining weight ever again. Be that as it may, if a craving does happen then enjoy it, because it means you have won, you are not doing the habit and therefore within a short time the craving stops. As mentioned, the primary function of the subconscious is to protect habits and by doing so it thinks it is protecting you. We know this because if pulled under the water when swimming, you automatically go to the surface and subconsciously swim, due to the protected habit of swimming. The subconscious is there to protect you, so with my help, using hypnosis, it will know that the habit associated conditioned links of snacking or overeating is bad for you is bad for you, and is no longer needed; it will keep you free from junk (poison) in the future. So with hypnosis we are going to replace the old habit with a new memory of not wanting to snack and take the habit of snacking away, we are going to get you to use your imagination to imagine so that it is easy to lose weight (easy to stop), then it will be. By doing so we are going to remind the subconscious that it has got to protect these new healthy associated links and habits. You now see how easy it is to lose weight (easy to kick the habit); it is a simple state of mind."

Dear student, basically explain the mind model to the client and cover the four reference points of the mind, and the seven mind rules were appropriate to their problem. There is one more thing to add to your script, with regards to the mind model. That is, the subconscious mind has no concept of time, so it will be easy to overcome the client's problem. You could say to your client:

"You see the human mind works by association. When we experience two things together for a little while, one (the anchor), will automatically remind us of the other (associated memory and emotions), in the future. That is also proof that the subconscious mind has no concept of time. Remember the subconscious mind reference point (C): "The subconscious mind has no concept of time, past, present or future." The associated links of memory and emotions to the anchor, will be the same age twenty years from now, the same age from the day you created the anchor, so you will still remember the event and (or just), feel those same emotions that you have associated to the song, as if you were back in that time, the day you created the anchor. This is due to the subconscious mind not realising that twenty years have gone by, it is as if it were yesterday. Your physical body has aged, but those associated links to the anchor, are the same age as the day they were created, and therefore the subconscious mind has no concept of time. This means that memories and emotions within the subconscious do not age, and also a memory and emotion are two separate things from the same event, hence why a memory can be repressed and the emotion be remembered. Why the memory can be repressed was explained in my Beginners to Advanced Volume One Book. Of course you consciously know past, present and future, but that is not where the associated links to the anchor are stored. A memory, emotion (associated links to an anchor), are stored within the subconscious. Even though a memory and emotion cannot be changed and are the same age throughout life, we can still create a new memory and emotion of the same event to the same anchor, in order to replace the old, via the subconscious, using hypnosis. This way we rationalise an event through an adult's perspective, instead of the child's old perspective, so that any negative effect that the associations to an anchor were causing, can be removed and replaced for new positive associations."

Dear student. In this script I am simply showing another way of explaining the information to make it more personal to the client's problem. Reading this script of ideas, you will realise that what the client is told, and what I have taught you to do as a therapist, the skills, the understanding of the client's problem and the way they think, and how I advise of how you need to think, are two very different mindsets. The therapist is using skills that the client is not consciously aware of, tone of voice, observation, building rapport, leading, etc. They do not know techniques like free association or the fact that you are bypassing their conscious mind via a TDS; they don't need to know your skills. As long as the client understands what you are saying, they don't need to know the real reason you say certain things, or your body language like the manipulation anchor at the beginning of this script to get the client to say: "Conscious Mind." That skill used both verbal and non-verbal manipulation that the client is not aware of consciously. All they need to know is the understanding of their problem, how to solve the problem and understanding their own mind. What the therapist is doing in the back ground is a skill the client will never be fully conscious of. You the therapist are in fact controlling two minds very differently, yours and the clients and yours will be always one step ahead of the clients, because you have the psychotherapy skill knowledge that they don't. So there is no need to fully explain what you are in fact doing to the client, just make sure that what you are doing works.

Metabolic Rate and Illness

Dear student, this sub-chapter I would consider to be a chapter to add to your weight loss sessions at a more advanced level, after you have gained more experience and confidence. The reason being is because you need to know how far you can lead a client without upsetting them in a negative way. This takes experience and skill of observing the client's body language in order to assess their emotional state of mind. From this sub-chapter all clients will be shocked and may even abreact so you need to learn from experience how to control their state of mind for a positive outcome.

This is done in the pre-talk. I always get the client to visualise a slim person in front of them with the same lifestyle, age and height as them, with the only difference between the client and the imagined slim person being that the slim person does not over eat. I ask the client: "Is your metabolic rate higher, lower, or the same as that slim person considering you are overwelght and they are not?" Some cllents may ask: "What Is the metabolic rate?" I reply by saying: "It is the speed at which your body burns off food and the rate at which your body works." However, most clients will say that their metabolic rate is lower than the slim persons, and they say that because it gives them a deluded sense of justification of being overweight, so they are blaming a low metabolic rate for their weight gain instead of taking responsibility for their overeating. The clients that don't say lower will say that their metabolic rate is the same as the slim person. I cannot remember a client ever saying that their metabolic rate is higher than a slim person because in their mind that would make them feel guilty, due taking the excuse of being fat away. The fact is the client's metabolic rate is more than double that of a slim person of the same age and height. This is because the client's body has to work twice as hard as a slim person just to keep them alive, even when they are at rest. Meaning their lungs have to work harder to take in more oxygen and their heart rate is higher in order to pump more blood and oxygen around a bigger mass, their body. Overweight people breathe in one and a half times more than a slim person, even when just sitting and relaxing, so it stands to reason that their metabolic rate is double that of a slim person. It must be emphasised to the client that this is just to keep them alive, because their body wants to, but is struggling to survive.

I then tell the client: "Not only is your metabolic rate double when just relaxing, but on top of that you are overeating, so your body has to work even harder to keep you alive in moments of binge eating or eating the wrong foods. Just walking upstairs you are out of breath, so of course your body has to work harder than a slim, healthy person's body." That information is a huge shock to the client and when done correctly it will have a positive effect of creating guilt in their mind towards overeating, you are using this guilt as a slow build up to leading the client to an abreaction that will come later if not already. You can then use that negative emotion and associate it to overeating within the client's subconscious.

There are web sites that you can add your details to, for example: height, weight, age and it will calculate your metabolic age. Your client may be thirty five years of age from birth, but due to the negative lifestyle they have been living, their body's metabolic age is that of someone in there fifties. Meaning that internally they are ageing rapidly and this will lead to health related problems like heart disease, strokes and diabetes in the future. The client must be told that their metabolic age can be reversed through simply changing their life style and by doing so it will prevent fat related illnesses. Your true age is always your metabolic age and birth age is really irrelevant when it comes to health and the age a person looks.

I continue by asking the client: "What is the number one cause of blindness?" Pause for a moment, and most will reply by saying: "Is it diabetes?" I reply: "What is the number one cause of diabetes?" Pause again and if the client doesn't answer then continue by saying:

"The answer is being overweight. So it is time to change, because blindness or blurred vision comes on average ten years after being diagnosed with diabetes, depending on the level of the illness, this is called retinopathy. Diabetic retinopathy is damage to the retina caused by complications of diabetes mellitus, which can eventually lead to blindness. Retinopathy affects up to 80% of all diabetics who have had diabetes for ten years or more. Despite these intimidating statistics, research indicates that at least 90% of these new retinopathy cases would have been prevented if there was proper and vigilant treatment and monitoring of the eyes, and damage to the eyes is totally prevented if the person looked after them self. Why take the risk of blindness when it is best to simply lose the weight now to prevent diabetes and retinopathy. Most overweight people over the age of thirty five, and depending on their weight, are five to seven years away from being diabetic if they continue the negative lifestyle. With that being the average rule, I have still known of a young girl in her twenties becoming blind suddenly, and she did not even know she was diabetic. She was on holiday with her friends, and during the time it took for her to walk from her hotel room to the swimming pool; she became permanently blind, for life. That is how fast blindness can occur with diabetes, due to the continued abuse of the body, and it was preventable. A male client of mine turned up for a weight loss session and he was blind in his left eye due to retinopathy, he described his eye popping one day and he had been blind ever since. A client's mother of mine had a daughter aged eighteen, and the mother book her in for a weight loss session appointment. The client was sixteen stone (two hundred and twenty four pounds). She did not turn up for the session so I phoned her home and the mother answered. She told me that the day before; her daughter had been rushed to hospital in an ambulance, due to being so ill. Her body had given up from all the years of abuse and due to not knowing she was diabetic, she had not been taking the correct precautions. This girl's quality of life is now seriously affected for life. Was that chocolate worth it?"

I then ask the client: "Why can you visually see all the fat around your chin and body?" The client may get confused at this point or be too shocked to reply. Please remember that as a therapist you are in control and rapport has already been established with the client, and that means that you are allowed to be direct with the client, so continue by saying: "It is because your body wants to survive, so it is pushing all the fat to the outer edges of your body. If it had not automatically done that then your heart and major organs would be surrounded by fat and you would now already be dead."

Dear student, when I say that, I push my hands forward as if pushing the fat, so that the client can observe in their imagination the fat, so that the thought of overeating becomes a negative act. I then pause, for reasons explained in the: "Verbal Psychology Chapter," in volume one, the interruption in the flow of language, both verbal and non-verbal, offer us the best opportunities for emotional communication. I am building on the guilt of overeating, so that later, under hypnosis, I can continue the guilt which will lead the client into an abreaction, in which I can then associate the neurological pain towards never abusing themselves again. I continue by saying:

"Isn't your body clever that it does that? It has pushed all that fat to the outer edges, because it wants you to survive and it is trying to protect you, but you are not helping yourself or your body with all the self-abuse. So you have a visual representation of fat that your body has shown you, to send you a signal to stop abusing yourself. And what have you done? You ignored that signal year after year. Your body has also given you heartburn and bad wind as a result of all that food and sugar fermenting in your stomach due to overeating and lack of exercise. Once again, you have ignored those signals from your body for years. You are out of breath by doing simple tasks like walking upstairs, and being out of breath is a signal from your body to lose weight, but once again you have ignored that helpful signal. Your body has told you that you are satisfied with the amount of food that you have eaten and you have once again ignored that signal. Your body then tells you that you are full, it cannot keep sending you the signal that you are 10% full, now 20% and so on, because it has already sent the signal and you ignored it to the point of making yourself feel sick, or bloated, or feeling like your stomach is about to explode. You simple walk around the shops and are out of breath from that simple exercise, and again your body is telling you that it cannot cope with everyday normal activities. At what point does your body give up, as you continue to ignore those signals, and you get a serious health related problem from being overweight?"

Dear student, again, shock sets within the client's mind for positive effect, so it is time for the client to start listening to the signals from their body. The client will at this point look upset, so I say in a harsh controlled way: "You are not here today to be told that everything is going to be alright, because you know what, if you continue as you are, then life for you is going to be devastating. I am telling you all this to save your life, I am giving you a reality check because it is what you need."

By saying that, you have also compounded the rapport between you and the client, because the client begins to realise that what you are saying is for their own good and so you must care. This builds transference towards you, the psychotherapist, and so the client will agree and be comfortable with you. Also at the same time, guilt towards overeating is building.

Chewing Gum

It is a known fact that when chewing gum the brain receives a signal from the body that you are eating when in fact you are not. This produces acids in the digestive system that burns off foods that would have ordinarily not burned off fast enough before the client's next meal, due to them not being active enough and having eaten too much. So it is important to advise the client to chew gum after a meal and throughout the day because that will help their body break down food, and therefore help them lose weight.

However it is advised not to overdo the chewing because the acid build-up can cause indigestion and stomach cramp, due to no food being consumed at the time of chewing. Also the body cannot function correctly without the right vitamins, so advise the client to take vitamin pills and drink plenty of water. Going off topic a little here, but out of interest I will share this information. Did you know that when we chew gum the brain increases blood circulation by 40%? This is of huge benefit when studying or wanting to concentrate more.

Eating More after Consuming Alcohol or Water

All weight loss clients, in fact most humans, cannot understand why they want to eat large amounts of food after drinking large quantities of liquids, for example: alcohol. There is an old wives' tale that says, when we get older we confuse thirst for hunger, and therefore if you feel hungry, just have a glass of water instead. People have believed that for years and all have been wrong and this is why. At one time it was thought that when we drink, the stomach holds this liquid and it slowly enters the digestive system. Hence the thought was that drinking would make you feel full because the stomach is full of liquid and therefore the brain would receive a signal that the stomach was full, so the brain thinks you must have eaten. It sounds like correct information, but I assure you it is very wrong. The fascinating fact is that when we drink, the liquid expands the stomach and then quickly (not slowly) leaves and enters the digestive system, and we soon need to urinate. You know the number of times you go to the toilet when out drinking, in the bars, or at home, so clearly the liquid does not remain in the stomach for very long. When drinking, the stomach expands in size due to the mass of the liquid consumed, and the stomach does not contract fast enough and therefore remains larger, even though the liquid has passed through. The stomach is now empty, because the liquid has passed through taking whatever food remained. This then sends a signal to the brain that you are starving, due to the stomach being larger and empty, so hence, the reason why we want to eat more food than normal after drinking, so the old wife's tale has always been wrong. That information must be explained to all weight loss clients, especially those that drink bottles of wine etc. So to stop clients from overeating due to drinking a lot, that type of client must stop drinking alcohol in large amounts. Some clients have a delayed reaction to wanting food after drinking, this is due to being drunk, so the brain is not functioning as it should be, so it cannot receive the signal that says I'm hungry. This client will feel even hungrier in the morning than usual. The fact that the brain is not receiving the signal is very worrying, because it means that long-term use of drink is causing brain damage. That information can also be used to lead the client to feel fear, which encourages an abreaction once enough fear has been generated from this continued association of fear that has been building within the client's mind. One of my clients said: "The next morning after drinking, I always eat a burger, because it helps with my hangover." Little did she know as to why she wanted more food than usual, until I educated her on the information I have just taught you, my student. You can also explain the following to your clients that eat too much due to drink. Experiments have been done with this. Two volunteers, both men of the same age, height, and weight, were given the same meal every day for a full month and the same amount of water.

Volunteer "A" drank the water then ate the meal.
Volunteer "B" placed the same size meal in a blender and added the same amount of water that volunteer "A" had consumed, and then he drank it as a smoothie.

This went on for a month and the findings confirmed what I have written about the stomach expanding etc. Volunteer "A" was hungry again just three hours after having his meal; this was due to the water expanding his stomach and the food not filling the expanded space. Volunteer "B" who had consumed the same amount of food and water but as a smoothie, was still satisfied and felt no hunger some five hours after. This is due to the water being enriched with food and therefore remained in his stomach longer, so that his brain received the signal that he was satisfied. Now you know why we feel hungry after being out drinking, and why smoothies satisfy us for longer periods of time and that is why a smoothie is good for weight loss.

Your clients are like volunteer "A" and therefore they will feel hungry more often and hence the reason they will want to eat more food. But by doing what volunteer "B" has done or stop drinking in large quantities, they will lose weight. I then continue the session by saying:

"Hypnosis is a great tool to help you get fitter; improve your eating patterns and in helping you lose the weight that you want to lose. I can help you with the programming within the subconscious part of your mind, but you have got to take responsibility for your conscious mind. It will help you if I show you how our minds are made up."

Dear student, I have used the word: "Our" above as in: "Our minds." I do this to continue the rapport I have built up instead of saying: "Your mind" to the client. That way both the client and I are the same as explained throughout this course. At this point I would give the client examples of excuses I have heard over the years, as a way of making it easier for them to discover their own, they will relate to a large number of them. I shared with you many excuses clients have said to me at the beginning of this weight loss section. Ridicule the excuses and not the client. Then I continue.

The Importance of Drinking Alkaline Water Hot and Cold

Dear student, this sub-chapter is for your information to help you, and it is also knowledge that can be adapted into the session for the client's benefit. I am not going to go into this scientific detail as that would be another book, plus I am not a scientist, so let's keep it simple and basic and if you need further information then please invest in a book on the subject of alkaline water or watch the many videos on Utube.

The "alkaline" in alkaline water refers to its pH level. The pH level is a number that measures how acidic or alkaline the water is on a scale of 0-14. For example: a liquid with a pH of 1 would be very acidic, and other drinking fluids with a pH of 14 would be very alkaline. As humans, we are alkaline beings and not acidic and our bodies are made up of over seventy percent water. Those people that drink acidic drinks like fizzy pop are generally more ill and look older than someone that drinks alkaline water of the same age. That is because illness feeds off an acidic body, the common cold and cancer for example or worsened by an acidic body. Just think how healthier you will be by changing that seventy percent water within your body to alkaline, the acids within you are neutralised, which leads to increased oxygen throughout your body and we know that increased oxygen kills bacteria's and viruses. Also an alkaline body improves energy and better metabolism and alkaline water contains antioxidants that are anti-ageing. You can buy alkaline sticks and drops to place in normal tap water to change its pH level to alkaline.

Drinking half a pint of alkaline water every morning half an hour before eating has been known to improve and even cure the following diseases:

headache, body ache, heart system, arthritis, fast heartbeat, epilepsy, excess fatness, bronchitis asthma, TB, meningitis, kidney and urine diseases, vomiting, gastritis, diarrhoea, piles, diabetes, constipation, all eye diseases, womb, cancer and menstrual disorders, ear nose and throat diseases and also high blood pressure is lowed.

I have treated many clients that just drink only fruit juice or fizzy pop drinks and they never drink water until I educate them. Only water will hydrate you and nothing else comes close for health benefits. I have personally known people with severe arthritis that have told me they are one hundred percent cured with a combination of alkaline water, health foods and exercise, and there are no side effects other than having to urinate a few times more each day, due to the three pints that are needed to be drank throughout the day. What is very important to note is this: you must drink hot or warm water soon after or during eating a meal and not cold water. The reason being is this: if you drink cold water whilst food is in your stomach then any oils from the food will solidify, which slows down digestion rate and can clog up your arteries, causing stroke or heart attack and therefore death. In an acidic body any solidified oils react to the acid and over time build up, which then turns into fat and that situation can lead to some cancers. So my advice is, drink cold alkaline water half an hour before or after food and never on a full stomach or whilst eating.

I have in fact been drinking alkaline water for a number of years, and from personal experience I can report that there is no question on the added health benefits, and as an added bonus I look younger, with a healthier, wrinkle free skin tone.

What Do You Know About Hypnosis?

Dear student, only say the following if the client is worried about being hypnotised, because the more they understand, the more they will relax around the idea of being hypnotised, because their negative worrying preconceptions are wrong. Continue:

Well, I cannot make you do anything that you do not want to do. This surprises some people because they see those hypnosis shows on the TV and it does make it look like they are making people do what they do not want to. Think about it, why do people go to see those shows? They go to be entertained, to see people act stupid. So then, they ask for a volunteer. Now who is going to volunteer? So the hypnotist entertainer has all these people on stage and he starts deciding who will be the most entertaining, who is the biggest show off. The people in the audience might be thinking that he is looking for people that are hypnotisable, but he is not, because he knows that anyone is hypnotisable, so he is looking for the biggest show offs, the ones that want to be the centre of attention, the biggest exhibitionists. Now he has got it made, he is not making them do something they do not want to do; he is making them do what they already want to do. And that is great because that is exactly what we are doing today. I am not making you overcome your past problem; I am helping you do something you already want to do. Hypnosis is a great way for getting you to do what you already want to do but couldn't, due to trying consciously. When you relax via hypnosis you will not fall asleep, you will be aware of everything. You hear the sounds outside the room, the sounds from in the room, you remember everything. You still have thoughts running through your mind, one of those thoughts might be: "Am I hypnotised?" Well the answer to that is yes, because hypnosis is a feeling of being relaxed, and because you are relaxed, I can talk directly to the subconscious part of your mind in order to help you overcome the past problem.

The best way to describe hypnosis is to say that it feels like first thing in the morning, you have just woken up but you have not opened your eyes yet, you know you can open your eyes if you want to, but you do not want to because you are so relaxed. You are going in and out of hypnosis all day long, without even realising it. The most common form of hypnosis is driving. You are driving down the road on a trip you have done a hundred times before and you start to daydream or think about something else. Next thing you know you get to your destination and you have no idea how you got there. That is: "Highway Hypnosis." Whilst driving, your conscious mind has wandered off and your more powerful subconscious has driven you safely to your destination, due to the habit of driving the same route many times in the past. Also, reading a book or watching the TV. You are at home and you are watching TV and you are hanging on every word that is happening. Someone asks you a question and you do not hear them, or you do not want to hear them, because you are so relaxed and don't want to be disturbed.

Now there are a number of ways to respond to hypnotic suggestions. For example: you could respond within your mind by thinking: "Yes" or "No." So if I make a suggestion of: "You are now ready to overcome the past problem" and you think: "Yes I am" then that suggestion will work, and it will work every time in working towards a positive result of achieving your goal. Another way to respond is to be uncomfortable with the suggestion. For example: if I say: "You are now ready to confront your fear" and you think: "No I am not" then that suggestion I made will be rejected, so you are in control at all times. I sometimes have people in therapy who have been sent to me by their husbands, wives, or doctors, and they say: "Get in there and sort your problem out" and like I said, I cannot make someone do what they do not want to do. So again the suggestion is rejected because that type of client is unmotivated, they do not want to overcome their problem. Another way to respond is to hope. Now, there is a problem with the word hope, it is the twin sister of the word try. If I try to pick up this pen up, I do not do it because I am just trying, if I want to pick it up I will. The subconscious is too busy doing a hundred and one other things to care if you are just trying. Therefore if you are uncomfortable, unmotivated or just hoping and trying then the subconscious has not got time to listen and so will just reject any suggestions. However by being motivated and wanting change for the better, and by you agreeing and liking the suggestions I give, and by you wanting this session to work, not only will the positive suggestions be accepted, they will also be acted upon.

Hypnosis is like a contract between two people. My part of the contract is to give you all the thoughts and therapies that I know are going to make you happier. Your part of the contract is to follow along with the suggestions, want them to work and allow them to work. Now I know I am going to keep up with my part of the contract. Are you going to keep up to yours? Good, then we are going to be successful.

Dear student, at this point you can do a suggestion test on the client as explained in the Volume One Book. This will prove to them how powerful the subconscious mind is, it also adds to the belief in what you have told them about the mind model. Have you noticed that the information just given in this sub-chapter contradicts what I have taught you? With regards to what is said to the client when talking about hypnosis, I wrote: "Well, I cannot make you do anything that you do not want to do." As a student you know that is nonsense, because under hypnosis or light trace we can instruct a person to do anything. Even though that is true, the client doesn't need to know that, because they would feel uncomfortable around you, so what was said was simply giving them a deluded sense of control, when in fact they are not. It made them feel comfortable around hypnosis and therefore the session can continue.

Then I continue after the suggestibility test by saying: "Do you have any questions before you start living the life you want?"

Induce Hypnotic Trance

Dear student, remember when inducing trance within your client, you must pause when appropriate, in order to allow the client's mind to process what you are saying, and this also allows them time to respond. I am not going to write when to pause in this Induction script because every induction is different, due to being personalised to the client. The feedback loop effect from observation is also important, monotone of voice and don't rush, simply talk slowly, in a relaxed manor, mirror their breathing at times, and personalise the trance from information from the pre-talk, all of which I have covered in Volume One. Continue:

As we begin you will take note of the different sounds in the room, the sound of my voice and thoughts or images that may drift through your mind and that is fine. It is now time to relax, please stare at the ceiling or light, take in a deep breath and relax as we release this breath. Continue breathing deeply and exhale slowly as you are learning to relax. As we continue here today, feeling peaceful, both you and I want to remain comfortable as you listen and concentrate on what I am saying, because what I say is important to you in achieving relaxation here today and your goal. Simply let go of all the tensions now and enjoy the feeling of being relaxed. Now you must remember, as we continue to breathe in deeply and exhale, that sometimes you can hear my voice, as you can now, and sometimes it may seem very quiet, and at times it does not matter if you cannot consciously hear my voice at all, because you cannot turn your ears off and therefore your subconscious mind will still be taking in everything that I say. You cannot turn your sense of taste, touch or smell off and you cannot turn your eyes off, you will simply closed your eyelids over them, because you cannot turn your senses off, you are always in control. Take in a deep long breath, and hold it, then in a moment breathe out, and as you do so, you are releasing all the tension from the past day, week, month and year, that you may have experienced. Now allow your head to stay where it is and start to look down, as if you are looking down at your feet, even if you cannot see them. In a moment I am going to turn on some relaxing music that is going to help you relax even more as we continue.

(Turn backing induction music on)

Allow any thoughts you may have to float into the distance, as you become more and more relaxed as time goes by. Your eyes are now becoming so tired that they simply close, and as they do, you feel even more relaxed. Allow yourself to go to (yawn so that the client can hear you because this creates sameness as if having the same experience), a sleep-like state, so that what I say will go deeper into your subconscious mind and this will prove to be one hundred percent successful for you, that feeling of relaxation is wonderful, and we both know how wonderful relaxation feels, as you drift deeper as we continue. You are going to relax into a level of relaxing that you have only ever imagined until now. The mind and body connections are very powerful and as we continue you concentrate on what I say, your mind takes in this information and your body reacts by drifting deeper and deeper into a sleep-like relaxed state. Every time you breathe in, you then breathe out all that past tension as it floats away into the distance; this guarantees your success here today. You are an intelligent person and I know this because you have understood everything that I have educated you with so far today; this also guarantees that you are able to achieve your goal from this moment forwards and you know you are now also achieving relaxation. It may happen slowly at first, each person is different and we all relax at different levels over different periods of time and that is fine. The beauty of this is that it is void of having to do anything, simply relax and let go naturally.

Deepening Trance via Staircase

Now going deeper into relaxation as we continue and you can still hear my voice, and in order to travel deeper into this wonderful sleep-like state, we are going to travel down, all the way down the staircase of relaxation within our powerful minds, this staircase consist of ten steps, see yourself right now at the top on stair ten. This staircase could be anywhere you want it to be, anywhere your imagination takes you, up in the clouds, in the park or anywhere you feel comfortable, like on the beach maybe or even in your own home, as long as you see yourself at the top, on the tenth step of the staircase of relaxation, then the location does not matter as long as you like the location. I am going to count down from ten to one, and as I do, you will imagine yourself stepping down each step with each number that I count down on the staircase of relaxation. For every step you take down, you will drift ten times deeper into relaxation, drifting deeper and deeper into a sleep-like state. And on ten, see yourself stepping, drifting, and floating down, all the way down to step nine going ten times deeper into relaxation with every step you take. Step nine drifting down with your whole body, sinking down, feeling heavier, and heavier as we step down to eight. And on eight, for every breath you breathe in and then out, you are exhaling all the past tensions as we allow you to drift deeper downwards into a sleep-like trance state. Stepping, floating down now to step seven, going ten times deeper into relaxation with every number counted down as we float downwards towards step six. And on six, every muscle in your body relaxing more, and more, getting heavier each and every time you breathe out, stepping down another step to number five. Continue to concentrate on my voice, allow yourself to let go because it feels so nice to relax more than you have for many years. And we continue to go down the staircase of relaxation to step four, feeling wonderful and enjoying this experience as it happens totally naturally, without any effort whatsoever. Step three now, see yourself floating down even further releasing all that past tension as we go, as you relax. In a moment we are going to reach the bottom of the staircase of relaxation, as we drift down to step two, and on one deeply relaxed, your whole body relaxed.

Continue by Deepening Trance Further via Bed Image

Now that we have drifted down the staircase of relaxation, and now at the bottom we can allow your body to relax even more, because I want you to imagine that there is a large comfortable double bed at the bottom of this staircase, where you are now. See yourself walking over to that warm comfortable bed, pulling the covers back and slowly climbing into that safe environment, lying down, pulling that warm blanket over you right now. And as you relax you take one last yawn,(once again yawn so that the client can hear you because this creates sameness as if having the same experience).And that sleep-like state feels warm and safe as we continue further into relaxation. Allow your mind to concentrate only on my voice at all times, as you enter that dreamlike state that feels so wonderful.

Continue by Deepening Trance Further via Body Parts

We are now ready to relax each and every area of your body, and we are going to start with your head area working downwards into relaxation. Each and every muscle in your forehead, right now relaxing, and your cheeks both cheeks relaxing, drifting down, feeling effortless as you continue to relax. Your jaw relaxing and eye lids are getting heavier and heavier, your whole face and head relaxing feeling sleepier, heavier, drifting down, and relaxing. Now moving down towards your neck area, relaxing, your head may drift to one side as you are becoming more and more tired and relaxed. Each and every muscle within your body is going deeper and deeper into a sleep-like state. You will enjoy this relaxed state as we continue, moving down, drifting down to your shoulders, both shoulders feeling limp as they relax even more, you now feel so lethargic, sinking down, feeling heavy as we move down both arms. Allowing them to go limp and drift downwards into a sleep-like state, sinking down into deep relaxation. Concentrate on your chest and stomach area, with each and every breath you breathe out you are sinking further and further down whilst enjoying the experience. Drifting down both arms, relaxing going limp and heavy towards both hands now, imagine all those muscles in each and every finger and both thumbs going limp, heavy and relaxed. (Add your observations of the client's hands and other body parts once mentioned.)

Feeling so tired and relaxed, it is so easy to achieve this relaxed state by simply allowing it to happen naturally and enjoying the relaxation as you breathe in and out relaxing more. Now from the top of your legs, as we work down to your knees achieving relaxation as you drift off feeling calm, safe, and warm. Downwards now, down both legs, relaxing down to your ankles. With every breath you take in, you then breathe out and sink even further down. Imagine your feet, allowing your toes to go limp, both feet limp, relaxed and heavy. All the way from the top of your head, all the way down to your feet, you are now deeply relaxed. And this feeling of relaxation continues as you concentrate on my voice, because what I say is very important to you, because it encourages your subconscious to remember that you are achieving relaxation, and by doing so you will also achieve your goal, for which you came here today.

Continue by Deepening Trance Further if Needed

We are now going to travel into a deeper state of relaxation from the count of ten moving down to one, and drifting ten times deeper, feeling more relaxed with every number heard being counted down. And on ten, drifting, and floating down, all the way down to a deeper state of trance. And on nine going ten times deeper into relaxation with every number being counted down, drifting down with your whole body, sinking down, feeling heavier, and heavier. And on eight, for every breath you breathe in and then out, you are exhaling all the past tensions away as you drift deeper downwards into a sleep-like trance state. Stepping, floating down now going deeper, going ten times deeper into relaxation with every number I count down, as you float downwards towards your desired goal and step seven, relaxing. And on six, every muscle in your body relaxing more and more, getting heavier with each and every breath, breathing out, drifting down towards number five. Continue to concentrate on my voice, allow yourself to let go because it feels so nice to relax more than you have for many years. We continue to count down to four, closer to the level of relaxation needed for success, feeling wonderful and enjoying this experience as it happens, totally naturally, without any effort whatsoever. Three now, I want you to see yourself floating down even further releasing all that past tension as we go, and relax. In a moment you are going to reach the desired level of relaxation as you drift down to number two, and on one deeply relaxed, your whole body relaxed.

Hypnotic Therapy Session Begins and Ends

Dear student, slightly up your tone from monotone to low volume normal speech, then continue:

As you sit, feeling drowsy and relaxed you continue to listen to my voice giving you all the positive suggestions that you require. As we continue you remain in the pleasant state of mind that you are now in. Remaining relaxed and peaceful, even drifting deeper as time goes by.

Your whole body developing even further those deep, relaxing, warm feelings from the top of your head to your feet. We are now going to expand upon this new knowledge that you have required here today, making this a permanent part of your new way of thinking. The negative past will simply evaporate like a cloud on a summer's day and a new you will start to emerge for positive effect. My voice may seem to fade into the distance at times, and other times you are fully aware of what I say, this is totally normal as you drift between different levels of trance. Everything I say will seep deep into your subconscious mind, and remain there for your benefit, so that you can act upon the positive suggestions from this day forwards.

Boost Confidence within the Weight Loss Client

The following is said: "You have come here today so that we can work together in helping you achieve your goal of being slim, fit and healthy and therefore happier. As we continue you can hear my voice as relaxation feelings gets deeper throughout all the suggestions I am going to give you. These suggestions are for your long-term benefit in making one hundred percent certain that your goal of losing weight is achieved, starting here today. You have started a new journey in your life that will reward you daily as your health improves by losing weight. Look at the achievement you have made so far, you have come here today and that was a life changing decision for you for the greater good of your quality, and length of life. We have understood one another and you have learned many things about yourself that makes this journey easy, far easier than you ever thought possible, because you now know that in order to achieve this goal, it is a simple case of understanding the past problem and controlling it through your powerful mind. You have achieved relaxation more than you thought possible, so think about all the other things in life that you can achieve by focusing your mind on a goal.

Your goal at this moment is to lose weight and remain slim, so that you can live a long, healthy, productive, happy life. This new positive, amazing journey starts right now, so that your new life can begin. Our human bodies are truly amazing. The body is capable of repairing itself, our bodies can lose weight once we instruct the mind to allow it to do so, and that is what we are doing here today. The suggestions you are about to receive will instruct your subconscious mind to allow this amazing, life changing experience to begin and remain with you for life, making it possible to remain fit, slim and healthy for the rest of your life. The suggestions will be taken on by your subconscious as a habit and stored away within the mind forever, for your continued success. The suggestions are part of the new you. These suggestions are so powerful; this experience is so amazing that you will never fall back to being the person that you once were in the past, where your weight is concerned. Hypnosis is a new experience for you, a new approach to achieving your goal and it is the most powerful and successful way of achieving what you desire. As we continue, simply feel your whole body drifting deeper into relaxation. For the first time in your life you will have a really good, positive approach toward food and eating, and as you initiate this good, positive attitude toward healthy food, enjoy healthy foods, and chew them for longer in your mouth. You will create a permanent, positive change in your eating habits. □

From now on, you will prove to your own satisfaction that eating just the amount your body needs will entirely satisfy you; just like drinking all the water you need as you listen to your body's signals. Instead of trying to kill your appetite, treating it as a friend, you are going to work within the framework of your inborn, normal reflexes, making a friend of your appetite, paying attention to it; for this is a good thing. Slim people have appetites, they pay attention to it. Attractive people have appetites, they pay attention to it. Hypnosis makes a friend of your appetite, rather than an enemy. In the past, you have only been paying attention to half the signal from your appetite. Namely, the signal that says: "Eat, I'm hungry." But now you are making a friend of your appetite. You listen to all of what your friend's advice is. When your appetite says: "I'm hungry" you then eat, and when the hunger feeling first disappears and your appetite says: "I'm satisfied," you stop. You stop long before you are full, because once you have a full sensation; it means that you have grossly overeaten and put on more weight. You should never want to feel full again. You see, you have not been paying attention to your appetite at all, because your eating has been driven by emotional, subconscious or conditioned reasons rather than hunger. It is always proper to eat when your appetite says: "I'm hungry." But you have been eating when you have not been hungry. You have been eating out of habit, when your body had no need for food. You have been eating to satisfy your emotional, subconscious or conditioned cravings. You have not been paying attention to your appetite when it says: "I'm done. I'm satisfied. Stop eating." You have not paid attention. Your appetite does not need killing off by not listening to the signal that you are satisfied, instead listen and take the advice of that satisfied signal for the benefit of your health and stop eating. Hypnosis helps you make a friend of your appetite, you are becoming more aware and you pay attention to the advice of your new friend and tune in on your body's signals and act accordingly to the message from your body. It is important that you will eat just the amount that your body needs to replace your energy stores for immediate use. It is important that you develop the habit now; that you are always going to eat when and only when your body needs it. Under hypnosis, we can reinforce the normal feedback mechanisms of your body, the checks and balances your appetite signals you when you need food, and that tells you when your body's appetite is satisfied.

Regardless of how strong this hypnosis may be, it cannot overcome basic instincts for survival. One of the strongest instincts is self-preservation. Surprisingly it is your great concern about being overweight that leads to sporadic dieting. This in turn suggests starvation, and starvation, in turn demands defence. It brings out the instinct of self-survival. This basic instinct is one of the reasons responsible for maintaining your excess weight. If you starve yourself then your body stores fat because it feels there must be a shortage of food, so never miss breakfast, because this is the most important meal of the day that will help you stay slim. Visualise yourself as the slim, attractive, healthy, person that you will soon be. As you begin to talk and act like that slim, healthy, attractive person, you will soon become with your new slim happy self. Overweight is not a dietary problem, but an emotional, conditioned or subconscious problem. You must resolve right now to give up dieting forever. You will form a habit pattern to eat all you need when your body needs it. Pay attention to your appetite, trust your own reflexes, and listen to your body's signals. You may lose weight slowly at first, and the excess fat will be burned away in due time. You are becoming slim, healthy, and attractive. You will feel wonderful in every way. The word diet and dieting will be removed from your mind and all the plans you may have had for dieting will be removed from your mind thoroughly. Because dieting makes you think of going hungry and giving up food, which in turn starts the anxiety about starvation, which brings forth the instinct of self-preservation and storing fat. So you are through with dieting; through with dieting forever. You will simply eat less of some of the food that you now eat and avoid some sweet, fatty foods altogether, like sweets and chocolate. You will eat more fruit and healthy foods to replace the junk.

Through hypnosis you are restoring normal signals from the body, by listening and acting upon the signals, that will keep you satisfied and bring into play that wonderful feeling of well-being. The word diet is a negative word; it threatens you with denial of food. Hypnosis is a positive word; it makes you relax, feel comfortable and alive. Diets fail; hypnosis succeeds. Diet brings about starvation which leads to overeating and obesity. Hypnosis brings about satisfaction which leads to relaxation and brings about a slim, healthy, attractive body, a relaxed mind and a satisfied spirit. The old urge to diet is now completely removed from your mind, because now you realise that the real answer is in listening to your mind and body. Understand yourself and control your subconscious mind, and listen to the signals from your body's appetite. You will concentrate and obey every suggestion I give you, for hypnosis is a positive approach. Hypnotic suggestions which you receive, will rapidly bring about a change which is necessary to ensure a permanently slim, healthy, attractive body, which you so desire to remove the depression. Each time you are tempted to eat or drink anything that you know is wrong for you, you will say: "No" and stick by it, because the rewards of becoming slimmer are more important to you than eating or drinking the wrong foods. The rewards of being slender, more desirable, sexier, are more important to you than drinking and eating foods that you know are wrong for you."

Dear student, the bulletin points I am about to show you must be said slowly to the client for them to repeat within their mind. Say each one at least twice, continue:

"I want you to think about and say these short sentences within your mind."

1) I am annoyed at myself for self-harming in the past which caused me to be overweight as I am now.
2) However I have learned from my past mistake and now I am moving forward with a positive attitude for life in a slimmer, fitter body.
3) I desire to become fitter and slender and from this day forwards I am.
4) I am becoming more slender and happy as a result.
5) My appetite is now easily satisfied with a much smaller quantity of food that I have become accustomed to eating.
6) I know that my body needs protein for strength, so I enjoy eating a small quantity of lean meat and healthy foods.

7) I enjoy eating green, leafy vegetables.
8) I enjoy eating all the right foods which give me strength and a proper balance of minerals and vitamins.
9) My body already has stored fat, so my body has no need for additional life threatening fat.
10) My body is now ready to use this stored up fat as energy towards a fitter slim body.
11) As this fat is used, I feel the way I want to feel; strong, energetic and vigorous.
12) My body has no need for more fat now; I have no appetite for fats, sweets and starches because they are wrong for me.
13) I am disgusted by the fats in foods, because fat only brings pain into my life.
14) I avoid all the wrong foods that I have always known are wrong.
15) My body has no need for life threatening junk foods.
16) My tastes correspond to the real needs of my body.
17) Food substances that are not needed are disgusting to me.
18) I am now finding a new pleasure in eating the healthy foods that my body needs.
19) I eat slowly. I take small bites; I relish each healthy bite as I chew it, giving my body time to feel satisfied.
20) I am now taking time to actually taste the flavour of healthy foods that I eat.
21) I am rediscovering and enjoying differences between healthy foods.
22) I enjoy the taste of the lean meat, and a very small quantity makes me feel satisfied.
23) I enjoy the taste of the leafy vegetables.
24) I enjoy the taste of skimmed milk which brings so many valuable minerals.
25) I enjoy the taste of fresh fruits and green vegetables.
26) I enjoy all healthy foods so much, that a very small quantity of them makes me feel satisfied, so I stop eating.
27) I am completely satisfied with the healthy quantity of food I eat.
28) I need no more food other than what my body's energy needs.
29) I am losing weight and feeling confident about being slim.
30) I am going to weigh (desired ending weight) because at that weight I know I am going to feel very much better and be much more attractive.
31) I am going to consume the excess fat from my body by walking and other simple exercise.

32) In ten weeks I am going to weigh (10 weeks times' lb. per week) pounds less.
33) In ten weeks I am going to weigh (10 week loss amount) pounds.
34) I do this because I want to feel stronger and more vigorous.
35) I do this because I want to be healthy with a better quality of life and a longer life.
36) I do this because I want to be happy for my family and myself.
37) I desire to be strong, vigorous and healthy. That desire is so great that it easily and subconsciously controls my appetite; and I automatically eat only the foods that my body needs, in the quantities that my body requires.

Pain or Pleasure Suggestion Techniques

Dear student, pain or pleasure techniques have now been explained several times in detail earlier in the NAC, timeline and aversion therapy chapters in the Volume One Book. However there are many more ways of creating neurological pain towards a bad habit. As a beginner start basic with your client, but at some point start to do the more advanced methods which require confidence and skill in your abilities of understanding people's abreactive trigger points. Different examples of pain or pleasure are shown in this weight loss script and the stop smoking script. You can adapt them to suit. The method I am about to show, I would consider this to be used at an advanced level.

Pain or Pleasure - Negative Future

"(Client's name) you have never watched yourself abusing your body as you have been doing have you? We know you have not, and due to you never having watched yourself overeating the wrong foods, you have, in the past, disassociated yourself from your problem, instead of doing the adult thing and confronting the problem for positive change. Today you have confronted the problem and that is a huge step towards to positive change, and now it is time to take a further leap forwards by seeing the real you from your past in order to fully change in the present. I want you imagine that you did not come here today, and therefore you continued to abuse your body in the future, with all that chocolate. You and I have never met, so you continue to overeat, and I want you to see yourself sitting at home now eating that chocolate bar at some point in the future, having never met me. Look at yourself sitting at home putting that chocolate bar in your mouth, watch all that fat entering your body, poisoning your body with disease forming fat. And you continue to overeat in the future, having never met me; you continue to justify your actions with those pathetic, childlike excuses that you have told me (repeat excuses to the client from pre-talk).

Take a look at how foolish you look as you continue to abuse your own body. In a few weeks or months from now your health begins to suffer as you continue to play Russian roulette with your life, having never met me. You have already told me that you are out of breath by just running upstairs and doing simple tasks (information from pre-talk fed back to the client). Being out of breath after simple tasks is your body's way of sending you a sign that it can no longer cope with all that fat. You have been ignoring that sign for years, making childlike excuses. At what point does your body say enough is enough? See yourself even further in the future, having never met me, and you have put on an extra forty two pounds in weight, because you continue to abuse yourself, having never met me, so you get so lethargic and out of breath as your health worsens.

You go and see your doctor, see yourself now sitting with your doctor, this is a future event by not coming here today, because you and I have never met and therefore you continue to over eat the wrong foods. You tell your doctor that you have been feeling ill, so the doctor does some tests and says come back in a week's time for the result. A week later you go back and your doctor tells you some bad news, you have diabetes and heart disease and therefore you could have a heart attack at any given time, but there is nothing the doctor can do for you because there is no cure, and you are given six months to live. Now see yourself returning home from the doctor's and as you enter your living room, you see your son (name) is there playing games with your husband (name). They both look up at you, and both can see that you look upset, so your son says: "What's wrong mummy, what's wrong?" You then sit down on your settee and take a close look at your son's face as you see the worry in his eyes. "What's wrong mummy, what's wrong? I love you mummy, please tell me what's wrong," he says. Now as you look at your husband and son's faces clearly now, you say: "I'm so sorry, so, so sorry I have let you both down. I have been so selfish stuffing my face, never once considering your feelings and I am so sorry that I'm not going to be there for you both in the future." Look at your son's face as he says in a concerned manner: "What do you mean mummy? What's wrong mummy?" He is too young to fully understand the situation, but he knows something is very wrong with his mummy. Look at the tears well up in (name husband) face as you tell him: "I'm so sorry, because I only have six months to live." You tell your son that you won't be there for him in the future to help him buy his first car. You won't be at his wedding when he gets older, because when eating all that junk food, at no point had you ever considered your family's feelings, due to your own selfish reasons.

Junk foods must have been more important to you than your own family, it must have been, or you would not have abused yourself with it. You have to tell your family that you have weight related disease, heart disease and diabetes, and you have six months to live. Just imagine how upsetting that would be for you and your family, how devastated you would be. See your son's face now as he breaks down and cries because his mummy has let him down. Money that you could have been enjoying with your son on holiday was spent on self-abuse. That devastating emotion that you are feeling right now (observation) is because that is all overeating will ever bring into your life. Devastation and disease (associating the emotion to the bad habit anchor). Is it worth it? Is that chocolate bar really worth leaving your son with the devastating memory that his mummy was so selfish that she never once considered his feelings, and she killed herself with overeating self-abuse? What a terrible memory to leave a little boy. Do you want your son (name son) to have to go to your funeral and be left with that scarred memory for life? Of course not (client's name) and that is why you have come here today. So that devastating image will never happen because you no longer need, want, or crave junk foods in any way, shape or form. You and I have met, and you are an intelligent person, so you know it is now time to throw that selfish part of you away in order to move on in life in a slimmer, happier way.

If you have a moment of weakness and overeat, you will feel ashamed of yourself and any food that you are overeating will make you feel sick to the core. And it will get to a point where you can no longer continue eating that extra food that your body does not need. You will also think within your mind back to that devastating image of having to tell your family that terrible news due to being overweight if you ever overeat again. (More excitable pleasurable tone of voice) but you do not want that to happen, so having realised that we have met today, move forward now and imagine yourself weeks from now. See yourself with your family and friends, with you having a clean bill of health and you feel better than you have in your life. You are so glad that you came here today, because your weight starts to drop off as of now. If you get withdrawal symptoms or cravings, it will be an enjoyable experience because it will serve as a reminder that you have achieved your goal in becoming a slimmer, fitter, happier person starting today, because today has been one hundred percent successful for you. You no longer need to overeat because you realise that you can now control your eating with the power of you own mind.

For you, the rewards of being fitter and healthier are more important to you than that chocolate bar."☐

Creative Visualisation of Removing the Past

"(Client's name) remain where you are now, sat peacefully feeling calm, and in front of you, within your imagination you are to imagine a television that is turned on with a movie of you in it. This movie is an old film of you over eating the wrong foods; watch this movie from the past, as you once were for all those years. See yourself eating all those crisps, chocolate, and takeaways, making you more, and more miserable as time went by, as you gained more weight. It is time to remove the past once and for all, and in order to achieve this goal you need to destroy the negative past. Having seen the past you want to remove it and so you are more than happy, and willing to destroy this past image. This television holds the bad habit and all the memories associated to it. In order to remove this bad habit from your life, you need to turn the volume control all the way down to zero so that the past bad habit can no longer be heard. Do that now within your powerful subconscious mind, and you also need to turn the contrast and colour all the way down so that the old negative image of you can no longer be seen or heard.

Even so the memory of the past problem is still in the television set, so it is very important that it is destroyed, once and for all, forever. So you now need to turn the power supply off to the television, which detaches the past, making it possible to move forwards in your life. Turn the power off to the television now which turns your past off. In order to make sure the negative past person, whom you once were has gone, you also need to pick up an imagined hammer and hit the television with all your force and power, continuing in hitting it until it is hundreds of pieces.

How you once acted and what you once did, abusing yourself with the wrong foods, that person from your past has now been removed, so you can now move forwards in life feeling proud and healthy. It feels so good to have gotten rid of that past negative person doesn't it? Send me a sign again by raising up a finger on the right hand to show me you have finished destroying the past negativity and it feels good. (Wait for the sign) we can now continue with the session, and that's fantastic."

Creative Visualisation of Future Mirror Image

"Now that the past has been removed, it is time to see yourself as the new you that you have become today, and continue to be in the future, having changed. Within the mind look into a full length mirror now and the reflection is that of what you are going to look and feel like in a few weeks from now, having lost weight. That is fantastic, look how good you now look as you see this future reality of an image of your slimmer self. Your skin tone has improved, your health in general, and you look slimmer, healthier and happier. Friends have been commenting on how amazing you look and your confidence has improved, you feel amazing. This reflection in the mirror is the person you are becoming, because the process of change has already begun within this session. This reflection is the person that you have always wanted to be, see yourself now stepping into this mirror, into your future, slimmer, healthier self. You are to feel and see yourself now as the person you have always wished for, and this is now who are, and over the following weeks you will become more, and more like your true slim, fit, healthy self. Your fiends will now say (client's name) you look amazing, they will compliment you and you will feel the pride of achieving your goal."

Improve Confidence Relevant to the Session Type, via a Thermometer to 100% Successful

The following can be said to your client:

Now (client's name), imagine a thermometer filled with water, you know what a thermometer looks like and this one has water within it that you can see through the clear glass of the thermometer. It has the numbers one to one hundred percent written on the glass of the thermometer from the bottom to one hundred percent being at the top. This thermometer represents your confidence level from feelings in the past towards your past low confidence etc. It may be set at ten percent at the moment; even so we need to achieve a level of one hundred percent for this session to be successful. So let's imagine heating up the water that is within the thermometer with a flame thrower. The water lever is at ten percent at the moment, making your confidence level ten percent, however by heating up the thermometer the percentage level will rise as the water heats up and therefore your confidence level will rise also. By heating up the water your confidence level starts to rise up and up, making your confidence level improve, and rapidly rising 20% 30% 40%. See the level of your confidence rise as you heat up the thermometer with the flamethrower, moving the level up higher and higher, improving your confidence level, and as it does move upwards it is getting closer to one hundred percent, you feel even more confident as the water level and confidence rises. Once the desired level of one hundred percent has been achieved, I want you to send me a sign to confirm that this confidence thermometer is at one hundred percent by raising a finger on the right hand upwards, this indicates to me that we can move on to the next part of this technique. (Wait for the signal then move on). Turn the brightness up in your mind so that you can clearly see the improved overall confidence level, and considering this thermometer is filled with water, and that water is now at one hundred percent representing your achievement made here today, it needs to remain there at one hundred percent. To do this we need to place the thermometer into the fridge freezer. See yourself now; picking up the thermometer and walking over to the freezer, opening the door and placing your confidence level of one hundred percent within the freezer, your confidence level is now frozen forever at one hundred percent and it will remain there forever because it is now frozen. Fantastic, feels good because you have achieved a lot within this session, and you have overcome your past problem, so that your new positive life can start today.

Associating Good Feeling to an Anchor

I now want to remember the memory of a time when you felt really good about yourself, we talked about this in the pre-talk when you were telling be about (use information from pre-talk and talk in an excitable positive tone), you feel really happy in that time so see yourself their now, relive it. And when you have that happy, emotional feeling from that past time, I want you to expand upon it, see the situation that you are in, and that wonderful feeling that is generated within you. The content details of the memory are not that important. What is important now for you are the emotional, happy feelings that the memory generates within you. (Personalise from information previously given from the pre-talk.)

I want you to really remember how you felt inside, those good, positive feelings, and strong feelings, confident and self-assured feelings and the laughter from that time. You can allow those good feelings to grow stronger and more positive whilst you take in a really long, deep breath, in through your nose, and now let's associate that good feeling to pressing together your thumb and the forefinger of the right hand, and by doing so you are making the ring of confidence, so that you are associating that good feeling to making the ring of confidence with your thumb and the forefinger which becomes the anchor. This is an associated emotion to an anchor, when we experience two things together for a little while, one will automatically remind us of the other, and repetition is the mother of success, so keep repeating this exercise over the following days and weeks, so that you are making the anchor of the ring of confidence with your finger and thumb into a signal to your subconscious mind to make you feel good, because that is the happy emotion that is now associated to the ring of confidence. So whenever you take in a really long deep breath through your nose and press together your thumb and the forefinger of the right hand, you are going to feel those good, strong, confident happy feelings once again, and you can feel these good feelings anytime you wish, anywhere, in any situation. Because these good, strong, confident feelings are becoming more and more a part of you and you are becoming that stronger, more confident person that will guarantee your success in achieving your goal of overcoming (whatever the problem was). And remember, anytime you want to feel even more confident, all you need to do is breathe in that really long, deep breath through your nose and press together the thumb and the forefinger of the right hand, and you will once again feel those good, strong, confident feelings filling your whole body in order to make you feel better and better. You can feel wonderful, calmer, more relaxed and much more confident than ever before. You know what it's like to feel those good, strong, confident feelings and you can really enjoy remembering and experiencing those feelings once again, which are becoming more and more a permanent part of you. Feels good doesn't it (suggested command and not a question). Send me a sign that it feels good by raising your right hand (this was using the anchor from pre-talk triggering the right answer). Of course it does because you just created a new more positive reality for yourself, and simply relax and put your right hand down now and that's fantastic. Work on generating good feeling and then press together the thumb and the forefinger over the next few days to reinforce the anchor trigger of good feeling, and see how real that associated anchor triggers the good feeling that can be used in the future whenever you need it. Any time in the future should you have a silly thought towards a past negative problem, simply do as you just have and feel good by saying no to the silly old problem, or use the anchor when in a bad situation to make you feel good, however right now, you can relax and let go of the ring of confidence, because it is not needed at this moment in time.

Post Hypnotic Suggestion

"It is now very helpful and pleasant to go back to the good feeling anchor that we created earlier, by making the ring of confidence once again with your finger and thumb. Make the ring of confidence now, and I want you to see yourself in that time once again, and feel how good it does right now, just as it did back then. We have improved your overall way of thinking here today for positive effect as of now and in the continued future. You know that you can use this ring of confidence whenever you chose to, making you feel relaxed and calm around any situation that in the past you had a silly thought towards. This wonderful feeling of being relaxed and comfortable is a simple state of mind that you can enter whenever you choose to, because we have proven here today that you can relax more than you have in many years and therefore you can relax again whenever you wish to.

You have now placed yourself in a positive reality and that old reality has now gone forever, this is due to the new understanding of yourself and the past problem. Your goal of becoming slim and healthy has begun here today and you can now move on with your life, free from that past overweight problem. All this new knowledge that you have learned today has been stored within your subconscious mind, and that information can and will be used whenever you need a reminder to help you through situations that you may find yourself in. All the suggestions your mind has taken in today are for the greater good for you and the people around you. You will act upon the suggestions you have received because you now know by doing so you will continue to succeed, and you know you have succeeded and will continue to succeed from this day forwards.

We have proven today that you can relax, without the use of drink, sleeping pills or junk foods, and this is an amazing achievement and a new beginning for you because you can achieve this same success each day at home. You have learned how powerful your mind is and you know that by focusing on positive thoughts, they will bring about whatever it is you focused on, in this case relaxation and weight loss, so well done.

Now that you have achieved what you have today, just think what else you can achieve in life. See yourself going out and meeting new people in your new slim body, feeling confident, powerful and enjoy the feeling because you know you are looking forward to doing new things. You are motivated to achieve whatever you want in life, going to the gym may be or walking in the country. Over the weekend you will take your children (grandchildren, husband etc) for a walk in the country, it will be fun and enjoyable and whilst enjoying yourself you are simply losing weight in the process.

I am going to give you a hypnotherapy audio CD that you will take home and it will help you relax the same as you are doing right now. You will play it once every day, from today when you have a moment to yourself, or even in bed tonight and each night. Work on the good feeling anchor every day in the future for the next thirty days so that it becomes a permanent positive part of you."

End Session by Waking the Client from Trance

"After the count from one to ten, you are going to awaken. This process will be slow, giving you time to come around into a fully conscious state in your own time. Once fully conscious you will be so grateful and relieved that your past problem has gone. You will also realise the amazing, positive change within yourself, because this has been a positive life changing experience for you. You have not been able to relax for years but yet you have come here today to a total stranger's home, and done what you thought impossible, relaxed. What you have achieved today is amazing; in many respects it has been a revelation for you. It has been achieved by a simple change in your though processes, it is a state of mind that will now remain with you for life, for continued success."

And 1 – All the suggestions I have given you today will remain with you for life because you know how beneficial they are to you.

And 2 – From this day and every day in the future, this new beginning for you will fill you with joy of achieving your goal here today.

And 3 – Every morning you will be so happy to have this new beginning free from your past problem.

And 4 – Each day that passes you will get stronger and stronger as that past problem disappears into the distance, gone forever.

And 5 – Remembering to work on that good feeling anchor that we have created for positive effect today.

And 6 – All this new knowledge you now have, you can and will adapt it within all aspects of your life.

And 7 – Today you have been able to relax more than you have for many years, proving that you can achieve anything once you focus your mind on your goal.

And 8 – Each and every area of your body feeling refreshed and revitalised, ready to start your new way of life.

And 9 – In your own time, when you feel ready, simply open your eyes remembering all that has been said today.

And 10 – Fully awake now feeling amazing.

Dear student, Give the client a hypnotherapy relaxation CD and tell them they must listen to it every day, or night, as a booster to the session for at least thirty days for added support. This also helps them to work on the anchoring technique.

Please note that in the weight loss script you have just read, I first educated the client on the different types of eaters and the mind model in the pre-talk. Throughout that part of the session I was building up rapport and due to the rapport I have achieved, I can then confidently start to encourage a feeling of guilt towards overeating by educating the client on their metabolic rate and hunger cravings from drinking, if they drink. This guilt is then compounded by finding out the excuses the client makes that they wrongly use to justify their eating or/and habits, that was associating neurological pain toward the bad habit, and I can later use that pain to easily lead the client into an abreaction to change what was once pleasurable, overeating, to being emotionally painful.

As the session continued, if the client was unsure about hypnosis I would explain as I have shown you from the chapter: "What Do You Know About Hypnosis." If an explanation is not needed then go straight into the suggestibility test. I then hypnotised the client and gave the client positive, ego strengthening suggestions on what they are going to achieve. By doing so I have mislead the client into a false sense of security in order to put their guard down, then with the client's guard down the pain technique that follows will have a higher impact and an abreaction will occur for positive effect.

The client is then told that we have met, so they feel relieved, as I then continued with getting rid of the past and then boosting confidence and good feeling anchor. The client is left on a positive high, feeling so grateful to have a second chance in life. I have one hundred percent success rate with this approach.

Also please note that other bad habits like smoking and drinking alcohol are also dealt with as just shown. However phobias, confidence, and some other types of sessions are very different in the sense of no guilt or neurological pain is used, and the good feeling anchor is at the beginning of the hypnosis part, not as you have just read, towards the end of the weight loss (bad habit) session. The reason for this is because phobias, stress, anxiety and lack of confidence are already painful to the client, so I need to make the client feel pleasure at the beginning of the hypnosis part of the session once hypnotised. Whereas bad habits are wrongly pleasurable to the client, so I need to change that for pain. So a different approach for bad habits to most other types of sessions like phobias or confidence is needed. Allow me to explain more. The reason bad habits use good feeling anchors towards the end of a session and not the beginning is because neurological pain to the bad habit must be associated first. You would never anchor good feeling towards recovery before the bad, towards the habit, because if you did then that good feeling anchor would be used by the client to counteract the pain section during the session. This would have an overall negative effect, because the session would fail due to the pain associated anchor not working, due to the good feeling anchor overriding the pain. Also it is obviously more beneficial to end a bad habit session on a positive associated anchor of the present and future of not doing the bad habit, by leaving the client on a high after the neurological pain from doing the bad habit.

Your Journey Continues as this Book Ends

DEAR STUDENT, our journey together is close to completion. However the journey never ends, because life is a journey and not a destination, and the same can be said for your growing knowledge. If anyone ever says they know it all, about any subject, then they are very wrong, because there is always more to learn. After years of experience, it took me a further three years to write the first edition of my book: "Beginner to Advanced Practitioner Training Course & Self Development in Psychotherapy - Hypnotherapy - Neuro-Linguistic Programming (NLP) - Cognitive Behavioural Therapy (CBT) Clinical Psychology Vol: 1". Ten years later I am still adding more information, as I also continue to learn from experience, and I continue to share it with you.

I have written four script books. Those being: Phobia - Confidence & Anxiety - Weight Loss – Stop Smoking. You may want to invest in those script books as well.

You may be interested to know that I am working on a series of follow-up books to compliment my "Beginners to Advanced Volume One Book". The next book, which is the second volume, is very different than the first. Allow me to explain:

The entire client examples in all the script books, and in volume one are real, although what I have not done here, or in the first volume book, is write word for word, from beginning to the end, the dialog from full sessions of what my clients and myself have said. Instead, I wrote small sections of sessions from my experiences, to explain techniques to you and how clients think. I also wrote scripts to give you different ideas of what can be said. One of those books you have just read. The scripts were written in a way not intended to be read out to the clients word for word. I simply wanted to show you different, basic beginners and advanced ways of conducting therapy, in a structured session that you can personalise to each client.

In the next series of books starting from volume two onwards, I have written in full detail what is said from recordings that I have made of real client sessions. So the follow-up series, of books, are client case studies with each book being a different client case. In those books I will explain in detail the techniques I am using and why I have said certain things to the client, and I will explain the client's reactions. The client case study sessions were conducted at an advanced level, because that is how I conduct sessions, and therefore those books are for students that have already read volume one, and not just a scripts.

For those wishing to buy the CD's that are mentioned in this book, they are available on one CD Rom for your computer and it has eleven audio hypnotherapy Mp3's with free copyright. This allows you to make copies on CD to sell to your clients to maximise your profits and to help the clients further. They focus on: Stopping Smoking, Losing Weight, Boosting Confidence, Stress Relief, Improving Study Habits, Focus of Concentration, and Pre-talk. Also an induction backing track with subliminal messages of relaxation is on the CD, and that you can play in the back ground as you hypnotise your client.

Simply go to: www.inspiredhypnotherapy.com and then click on the: 'Prices & Online Store' page. You can also contact me through the web site if you wish to have personal training from me.

For those students that have studied this book as a Home Study Course, if you wish to take the Diploma exam, then the option to do so is available as shown on my web site: www.InspiredHypnotherapy.com on the page: "Prices & Online Store". The exam is done in your own free time from the comfort of your own home. You simply email me your answers. Students that pass will receive a Diploma Certificate, as shown on the web site.

Please add me on Facebook – 'David Glenn - Psychotherapy NLP CBT Hypnotherapy'. I am building a community of like-minded people, including my past students. I will post information on my new published books, and we can all help one another with questions and answers regarding psychotherapy as a whole.

Dear student, if you have any questions you want answering to further your knowledge, or you simply want to talk, then please phone me. Phone calls are free via Wi-Fi on WhatsApp from anywhere in the World. Telephone 07973481786

Of course I have to charge for my time. Those charges being £25 for half hour or less. Or £45 for over half an hour to an hour. We can cover many topics in that time. Payment must be made online before the call is made in order to schedule a time and date for our conversation.

I also conduct therapy sessions over the phone if you, or someone you know can't travel to see me in person at the same cost.

Simply email me your details, how much of my time you wish to have, dates and UK times that you are free to talk, and I shall email you a request for payment and set scheduled session. Alternatively in person I charge £95 for a full one and a half hour session.

david.glenn.psychotherapy@gmail.com

Dear student. Can I please ask for a few moments of your time to leave positive feedback on the site where you invested in this book? Without feedback, my time writing will have been wasted, because few people will invest in the book and I simply want to help people to study, to help others, and also for people to overcome their personal psychological problems.

Please note that I am not a professional writer. I am a therapist. Even so, I have done my best to write this book to help others and you. So please excuse the odd grammar error or spelling mistake. This book has been written in UK English and not American-English and for that reason many words are spelt differently to what our American friends are used to.

Thank you!

Dear student, I wish you all the happiness in the world and good health, until our paths cross again in 'Volume One or Two or more' or another script book. Bye for now.

www.ingramcontent.com/pod-product-compliance
Lightning Source LLC
Chambersburg PA
CBHW062017280526
45787CB00005B/2142